HORROR MOVIES

The Movie Treasury

HORROR MOVIES

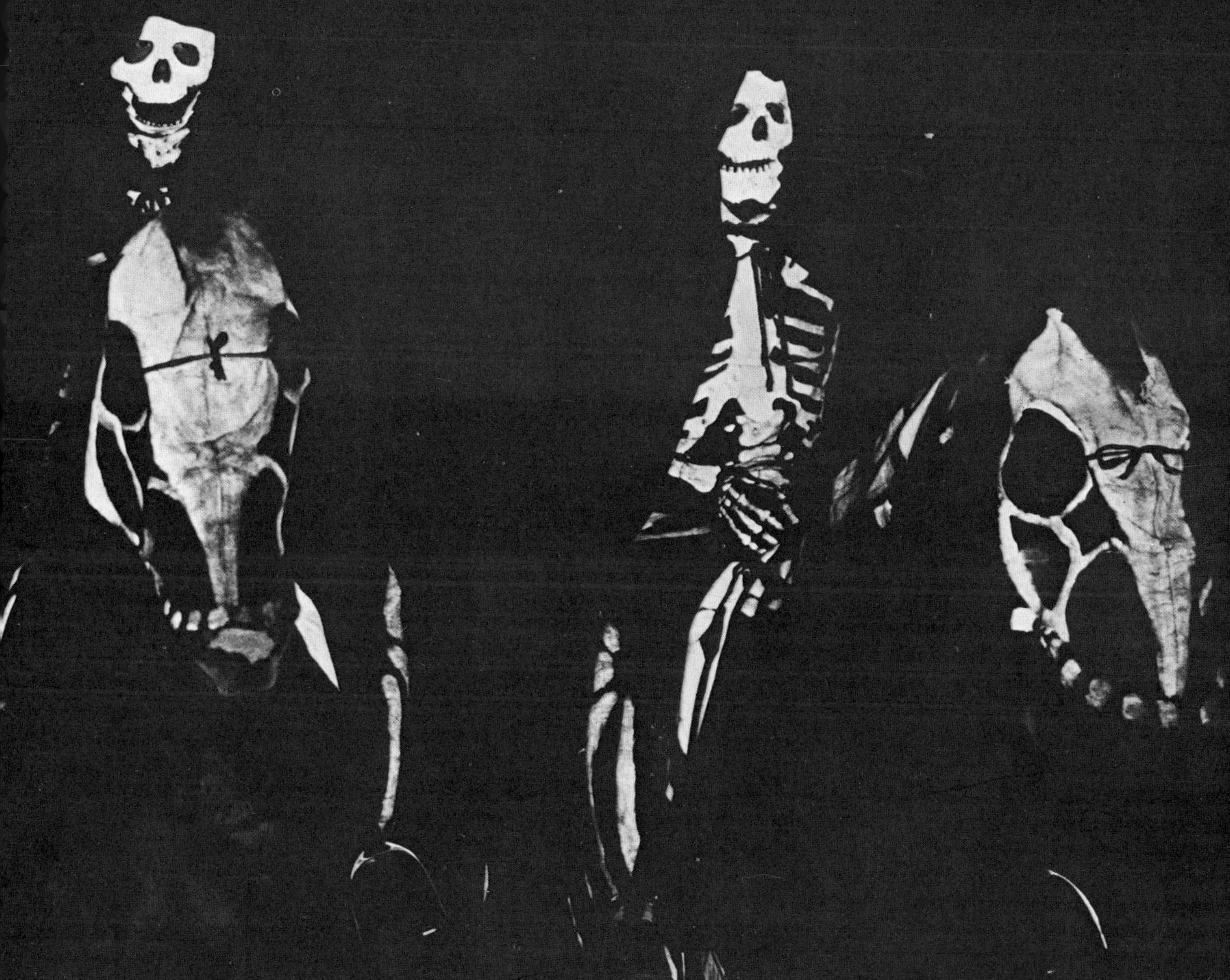

Tales of Terror in the Cinema

ALAN G. FRANK

Cathay Books

CONTENTS

NOTE *The dates of films given throughout this book are approximate. This is because of varying lengths of production-period, the intervals between production and distribution and differing dates of distribution in various territories. In most cases the date given is the year of principal production.*

INTRODUCTION

Horror films are one of the first genres to emerge in the cinema, and one of the longest lived. Even today, when the production of almost any kind of film represents a very real risk of commercial disaster for film makers everywhere, screen horror is alive and well and flourishing triumphantly in cinemas all over the world!

There is one basic reason why horror films have stayed popular. Throughout their 70-odd years, they have always managed to give their audiences what they wanted—pleasurable terror, and by so doing, have remained critic proof despite critical attacks or total indifference. We enjoy being terrified from the safety of our cinema seats, secure in the knowledge that the most terrible monsters that erupt across the screen are made 'real' only by our willing suspension of disbelief.

In providing generations of fans with the brand of terror they wanted, horror films—more so perhaps than any other type of film—have proved the truth of Adolph Zukor's dictum: 'The public is always right!' From the flickering demons and dancing skeletons created by Georges Méliès in the cinema's infancy, to the very latest nefarious deeds of Messrs. Price, Cushing and Lee, the monsters of terror that have stalked cinema screens have continued to find new and willing 'victims'. Every age of the cinema has had its horror 'greats', and in these pages we shall meet them all: the first team of Lon Chaney Senior, Boris Karloff, Bela Lugosi, Lon Chaney Junior, Vincent Price, Peter Cushing and Christopher Lee, along with their stalwart supports in monstrosities—John Carradine, Lionel Atwill, George Zucco, Claude Rains, King Kong, The Incredible Two Headed Transplant and a monstrous cast of many more!

I admit quite freely to being an addict of horror films, and, like all addicts, I hope that what follows will go some way towards introducing you to the many and horrible pleasures of this addiction. It is an addiction that is quite harmless: speaking of horror films, and who better to pronounce upon them, Vincent Price has said: 'Of course, over here (United Kingdom) all our films are "X" certificate. In America, on the other hand, they're released to coincide with school holidays!' And, on another occasion, Mr. Price remarked: 'I believe that horror is much less harmful than violence in films. I'm quite serious about the films I make. They are pure escapism and therefore harmless. No one believes them or takes them seriously.' And I, for one, would be unwilling to argue with Mr. Price!

As to an exact definition of horror films, here I must take refuge in knowing, along with fellow addicts, just what constitutes a horror film, without being able precisely to define those elements. In the United States, horror of the sort we shall meet with in these pages was never the subject of censorship—the Censors there were far more concerned with sex and the possible contamination of audience morals than with the unlikely goings on that took place in horror films. In Great Britain, the British Board of Film Censors did, in 1937, introduce their 'H' for Horrific Certificate. Without defining just what constituted a horrific film, their 'H' Certificate, until its demise in 1951, prohibited anyone under the age of 16 from seeing films so designated. Only 37 'H' Certificates were issued by the Board during the life of the 'H' Certificate, which was finally replaced on January 1, 1951 by the 'X' Certificate which rated all films of an adult nature, including with horror such elements as sex and savagery. Clearly certificates from censorship boards merely tend to categorize certain horror films, without defining them and, in the early days of Hammer Horror, varying versions of horror would be filmed

TOP LEFT *Boris Karloff, the gentleman of horror*
TOP RIGHT *Christopher Lee as Count Dracula with Caroline Munro in* Dracula A.D. 1972 *(Hammer 1972).*
FAR LEFT *The priest, Michael Hordern, stakes a burning cross through Baron Zorn's heart in* Demons of the Mind *(Hammer-Godwin 1972).*
LEFT *Peter Cushing, archetypal vampire-killer in* Dracula A.D. 1972.

Lee and Cushing (above) *fight the evil eye, and the lady* (below) *meets the railway monster on a one-way ticket in* Horror Express *(Scotia Int. 1974).*
Peter Cushing as Dr. Schreck (right) *tells the Tarot cards of death, and Death* (overleaf left) *awaits the travellers at the end of the line in Freddie Francis'* Dr. Terror's House of Horrors *(Amicus 1964).*
With curses and incantations Margaret Leighton as Madame Orloff (overleaf right) *battles with the unseen elemental on Ian Carmichael's shoulder in* From Beyond the Grave *(Amicus 1974).*

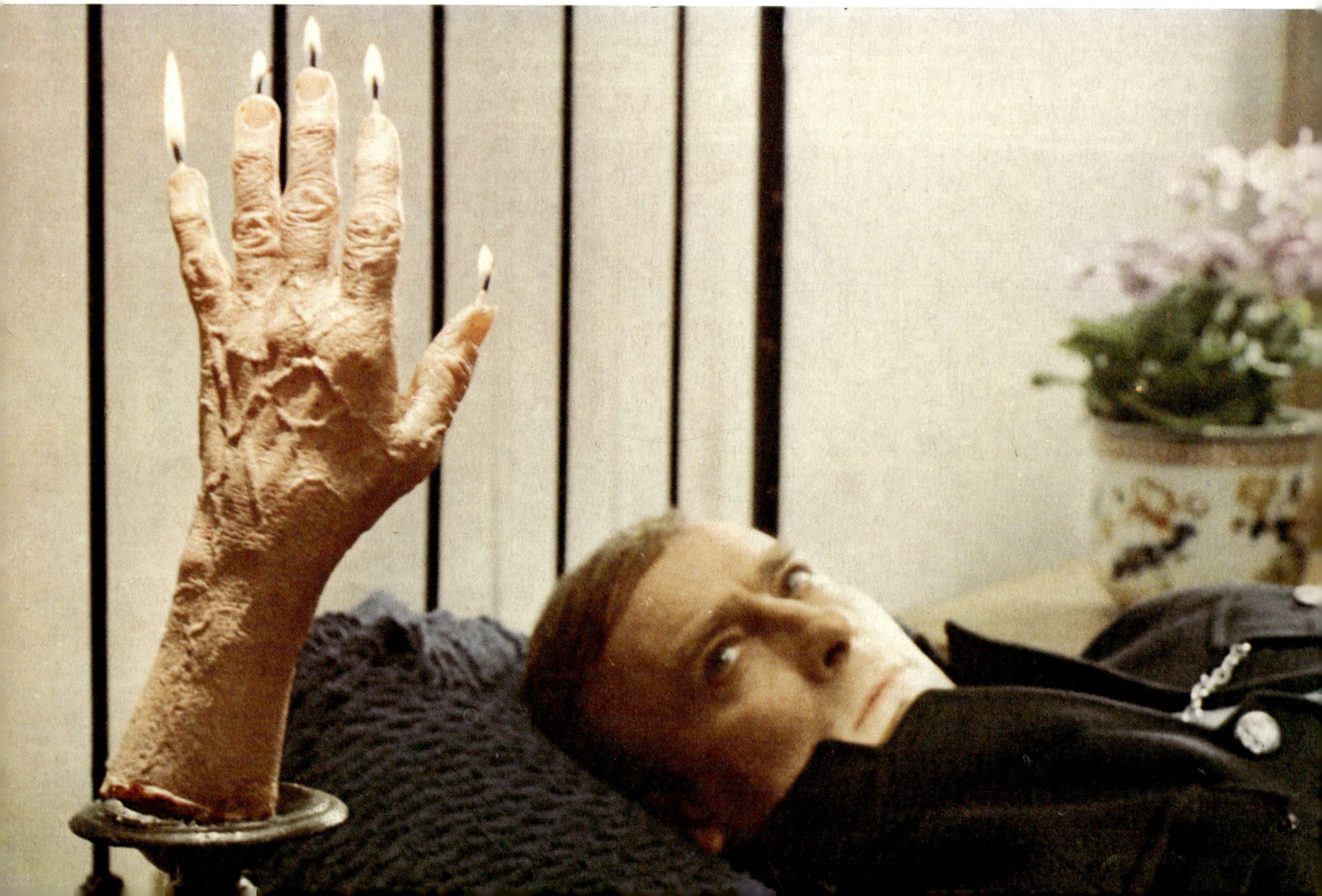

for each key scene; the British, the more horrifying American version, and then the ultimate for the Japanese, who were happy to take all the horror that was thrown at them! The fact is that what constitutes a horror film has little to do with any prevailing climates of censorship or morals. All of us possess within us a knowledge of what we find frightening, and it is that very personal knowledge that gives us all our own personal definition of screen horror.

Indeed whatever may scare one cinemagoer can well induce helpless mirth in another. As Dilys Powell, the distinguished British film critic wrote: '. . . one man's frisson is another man's guffaw'. Sir James Carreras, the man who made the name Hammer synonymous with horror in the Fifties and Sixties, has gone on record as saying: 'The wicked fairy in "Snow White"—she's much more frightening than any of our people' and Vincent Price agrees: '. . . *Snow White and The Seven Dwarfs* was one of the most frightening films I ever saw'.

For purists, here is the definition of the horror film from the Penguin English Dictionary: 'Film treating gruesome, terrifying or supernatural subjects in a sensationalist way.' In these pages we shall meet some of the staple films of the horror-fantasy-terror genre. We shall become familiar with a variety of vampires, the many creations of Frankenstein, werewolves, zombies, mummies, the undead and the reanimated, the ladies of horror and the madmen, the deranged doctors, mad scientists and their terrible deeds. We shall find sinister creatures of the night of every sort, the gigantic and the grotesque, freaks and hunchbacks, and the assorted demons, fiends and kobbolds that are the stars of horror films. As an aficionado, I hope that the following pages transmit some of the immense pleasure I have gained from years of tracking down rare horror movies in fleapits in Kenya, bio-cafes in Cape Town, some Trinidad cinemas even more frightening than the films they were showing, as well as the many British cinemas which revived screen horror on Sundays, with a double dose of enjoyable terror for the price of one film.

Inevitably, I shall offend some readers by leaving out their personal 'classic' horror films: others no doubt will want to take issue over the selection of films included. Naturally, I have had to be selective and my selection has been a personal one, and a painful one as space has forced the exclusion of many films and happy moments of horror. If I have offended, might I plead, in true horror-victim style, that rather than sinking your fangs into my neck in revenge, you write to me care of my Publishers.

ABOVE LEFT *Jack Watson, writhing and mutilated, perishes as the room disintegrates around him in* From Beyond the Grave *(Amicus 1974)*.
LEFT *Edward Woodward surveys his 'bedside lamp' with horror in* The Wicker Man *(British Lion 1973)*.
RIGHT *Mad scientist Peter Cushing in* The Creeping Flesh *(Tigon British/World Film Services 1972)*.

THE BARON

"I always saw my monster as something inarticulate, helpless and tragic. To him, Frankenstein was God." Boris Karloff

THE MOST famous monster ever to appear in the cinema began his life as the nameless creation of eighteen-year-old Mary Wollstonecraft Shelley, the second wife of the poet Shelley, in her novel of Gothic horror 'Frankenstein; or, the Modern Prometheus'. Written in 1816, during a summer the Shelleys spent in Switzerland with Lord Byron and John Polidori, *Frankenstein* is the story of a man who took upon himself the power that was God's and attempted to create life, only to be destroyed by the very creature he made. The moral was obvious, although little of this judgement was to carry over into the many films based upon the novel. Nevertheless, since his first screen appearance in 1910 in Thomas Edison's *Frankenstein*, through his many and various mutations on the screen up to the recent production of *Dr. Frankenstein*, the Monster without a name has terrified and gripped the imaginations of countless cinema audiences, and created two stars of the Horror Film, Boris Karloff and Christopher Lee.

The first screen version of *Frankenstein*, starring a Mr. Charles Ogle as the monster, seems to have been too weird for the taste of filmgoers in 1910. With the exception of one film in 1915 in America on the man-made monster theme—*Life Without Soul*—the cinema had to wait until 1931 for the great classic horror film *Frankenstein* with Boris Karloff as the definitive Monster.

The success of the film of *Dracula* in 1931 inspired Universal Pictures' decision to film *Frankenstein*. Carl Laemmle Jr, the son of the founder of Universal Pictures, hoped that Bela Lugosi, the star of *Dracula*, would repeat his success by playing the Monster in *Frankenstein*, and while *Dracula* was still in production, Lugosi was made up as the monster and photographed for the part. Edward Van Sloan, who took part in the tests, remarked that 'he looked like something out of *Babes in Toyland*!' Not surprisingly, Lugosi refused to play the Monster, claiming that the make-up would make him unrecognizable and, in any case, he did not want to play a role without dialogue.

The film was then given to British director James Whale, who having settled upon Colin Clive to play Frankenstein, looked among the players and extras on the Universal studio lot for someone to play the Monster. Whale had noted the work of a British actor, then working in a gangster film called *Graft*. His name was William Henry Pratt, but taking his mother's maiden surname, he acted under the name of Boris Karloff. He had made his first stage appearance at the age of nine in the singularly prophetic role of the Demon King in 'Cinderella'. Having abandoned a Consular training, Karloff made his first film appearance in 1918 in a crowd scene, going on to build his reputation as an actor in 'heavy' parts in silent and sound pictures. He was already 44 years old when Whale selected him to test for the part of the Monster. Whale, a former cartoonist, had started to draw and create an image of the Monster, taking Karloff as his starting point. He wrote: 'Karloff's face fascinated me. I made drawings of his head, added sharp bony ridges where I imagined the skull might have joined.' Karloff endured hours of experimentation as Jack Pierce devised and created the make-up that was to make Karloff a star for the rest of his life.

In the film, Frankenstein was to construct the Monster from pieces of human corpses and Pierce appreciated that it should obviously be the result of spare-part surgery.

To make the Monster's appearance medically plausible, Pierce studied anatomy, surgery, criminology, ancient and modern burial customs and particularly electrodynamics, since the Monster would ultimately be brought to life by electricity. Distinctive metal studs were inserted in each side of the Monster's neck—electrodes through which would flow the electric current destined to give life to the monster.

The make-up that finally emerged was so successful that Universal copyrighted it—thus forcing Hammer Films to create an entirely different concept of the Monster when they made *The Curse of Frankenstein* in 1957. But even with the addition

LEFT *The Universal Monster—Boris Karloff in* Frankenstein *(Universal 1931).*

of colour, they could not quite match the effect of the Pierce/Karloff creation. The terrifying face, overshadowed by a Neanderthal brow almost as high again as the distance from chin to eyes, was topped by a flat helmet of dark lifeless hair. Under the cliff of the brow were drawn cheeks, heavy eyelids coated with wax, and a black line of a mouth subtly contorted with unseen wire clamps. Gone was the gaunt and dark type of make-up that had prevented much expressiveness on the part of Lon Chaney. Karloff's face below that huge built-up cranium was infinitely sensitive, able to convey far more without dialogue than many later actors who had the added advantage of speech to help their horror characterizations. Finally, Pierce experimented with make-up so that Karloff's skin photographed as grey and bloodless as a corpse. The hands and fingers seemed unnaturally long, white as death, with suture marks at the wrists showing clearly to suggest Frankenstein's assembly, and the sleeves of the jacket were shortened to make the arms appear longer.

To make walking unnaturally difficult and to add height, Karloff was given a five-pound steel spine and large asphalt-spreader's boots (weighing 18 lbs), while his legs were stiffened by steel struts. When he added his considerable acting talent to the make-up man's art, the greatest film monster of them all was created. A monster which, for all the horror of its actions and its mis-shapen body, was still recognizable as having been created in the image of man. Greater mystery was added to the film by the suppression of Karloff's name until the film was released to incredible success at the box office.

The original plot had been made even more effectively horrifying through a brilliant addition to the plot by Robert Florey. Instead of the brain Frankenstein had intended to put into his monster's skull, the brain of a maniac is substituted in panic by the assistant who had dropped the original brain. The film monster now became a deformed parody of a man's body housing the brain of a madman. The monster, though little more than an animal, appears almost human, crying out for sympathy, despite its murderous activities.

The film is set, in the best tradition of the genre, in a village of that mythical part of central Europe where all the vampires, werewolves and mad scientists flourish. Outdoors, the scenes are austere, even surrealistic, with a vivid sky lowering over cemeteries, open wastes of rock and barely living plants.

Having been expelled from medical school for his strange and heretical beliefs Frankenstein has set up his laboratory in a mouldering tower. With his mentally defective hunchback assistant (Dwight Frye), he goes about the grisly business of robbing graves and gallows to get the various bits and pieces of cadavers needed to construct his creature. The Monster is put together surgically, and in a climactic scene that still retains its original power, is given life.

The body of the lifeless Monster lies waiting on the operating table, sheeted and bandaged, as an electrical storm rages around the laboratory tower. As the lightning flashes and thunder roars to a crescendo, the dynamos and electric arcs roar and flash in counterpoint. The operating table with the Monster strapped to it slowly rises to the roof which lies open to the 'life-giving' forces of the electrical

ABOVE *Monster 1970-style. Dave Prowse in* Horror of Frankenstein *(Hammer/EMI 1970).*
TOP RIGHT *Dr. Frankenstein (Leonard Whiting) works on his creature in* Frankenstein, The True Story *(Universal 1974).*
RIGHT *Karloff in a lakeside idyll with Marilyn Harris—the flower that wouldn't float—in* Frankenstein *(Universal 1931).*

ABOVE *Baron Frankenstein (Colin Clive) and Fritz (Dwight Frye) prepare to make a monster in* Frankenstein *(Universal 1931).*
BELOW *The Monster carries on into the Seventies with* Blood of Frankenstein *(Independent-Int./Paladin 1972).*

storm. Then, as the storm subsides, the table is slowly lowered, and the cinema's greatest monster is born to Henry Frankenstein's triumphant cry of 'It's alive. It's alive!'

His triumph however turns to revulsion at the sight of the monster he has brought to life. Sickened by the face of the Monster, the pathetic, almost childlike movements of his hands towards the light that enters the cell, and by his stumbling semi-human, semi-robot movements, Frankenstein abandons the creature, chained up in a dungeon, to the hunchback's attempts to tame him with flaming torches.

Nothing transcends those first scenes of Karloff where he plays the new-born monster, reacting to the stimuli around him in the pathetic manner of a backward child. Finally breaking the chains binding him to the wall, the Monster hangs the hunchback and escapes from the tower. In a scene of strange beauty, he comes upon a child by the side of a stream, and for a brief time, child and monster play together. The girl throws a flower to float on the river and encourages the monster to copy her. He does so, and then joins with her in play. One after the other, they happily take turns in throwing flowers to float away down the stream, until the

ABOVE *Karloff* (left) *made the Monster uniquely his own in* Frankenstein *(Universal 1931), and with Valerie Hobson* (right) *in* The Bride of Frankenstein *(Universal 1935).*

Monster innocently throws the girl herself into the river, and is saddened when she sinks and drowns. The game is over; now the camera tracks with the girl's father, striding through the village and carrying in his arms the pathetic soaking body of the dead child.

The film builds up to its final climax as the Monster is hunted by torch-carrying villagers, baying dogs and by Frankenstein. It ends with the Monster picking up Frankenstein and taking him to the supposed sanctuary of a windmill. The villagers follow and, determined to rid the world of both Monster and maker, set the windmill alight. The final fight between Frankenstein and the now totally crazed Monster in the blazing windmill, ends with the Monster hurling Frankenstein from the top of the pyre. His fall is broken by one of the arms of the windmill, while the monster is assumed to have perished in the flames. Shot against the leaden grey of a studio sky, the final scenes achieved a power to terrify that could never have been matched in colour. Some prints of the film were shown with a green tint which added to the horror of the Monster's appearance.

But what undoubtedly makes *Frankenstein* great is Boris Karloff. Although many other actors have played the part of the Monster—Lugosi, Lon Chaney Jr, Glenn Strange, Christopher Lee, Michael Gwynn, Kiwi Kingston and Freddie Jones—Karloff is the archetypal Monster, carving with his portrayal of the creature an enduring place in cinema history. His was a Monster of incalculable evil and terror, yet capable of moments of sheer pathos. A critic in the early 1930s wrote: 'Mr. Boris Karloff makes you feel that the Monster is not simply a mechanical fiend animated by a lust for murder. He gives the monster a soul . . . the amazing thing is that this creation in some way inspires you to pity.'

Frankenstein became one of the great horror films, setting a standard for all subsequent films, and Universal made advertising history by being the first (though by no means the last!) film company to scare audiences into the cinema by warnings that the film was not for the frail in heart. The company were soon to realize that the Monster's death had been vastly premature, and in 1935 Karloff and Whale made *The Bride of Frankenstein.*

The only problem, if problem existed, was to account for the Monster's reappearance, since at the end of *Frankenstein* he had been seen to die in the flames of the burning windmill. A happy epilogue in which Frankenstein, restored to health after his descent from the windmill and being wished well by his father, was removed from prints of the film in circulation, to make way for the revival of the Monster.

In a carefully contrived prologue, Mary Shelley (played by Elsa Lanchester, who was also to double as the 'bride') is seen discussing her book of *Frankenstein* with, among others, Lord Byron, who particularly wishes to hear more of the Monster. Mary reveals that instead of burning to death, the Monster was saved by falling through the flames into the flooded cellar of the mill, thus eluding both the pursuing villagers and incineration. *The Bride of Frankenstein* is under way.

The Monster is rescued by the parents of one of his victims who themselves perish. The Monster, his arm burned, tries to soothe it in a pond and so scares a shepherdess that she falls into the water. Not surprisingly, her rescue by the Monster does nothing to still her screams, and villagers arrive and shoot Karloff in the arm. Pursued through a forest of dead trees, the Monster is captured and chained to a huge throne in the dungeon of the local gaol. He escapes by snapping his bonds, and finds human understanding and comfort in the hut of a blind recluse. The Monster learns a few words, is fed on bread and wine and listens with near rapture to the violin playing of the hermit, This brief interlude is shattered when a traveller intrudes into the cottage. Within moments the hut is ablaze, the traveller and the blind man dead in the flames.

The Monster flees the scene of his carnage, through a graveyard and into a catacomb where the bizarre Dr. Praetorius is dining off a coffin. The Doctor, who is played by Ernest Thesiger, is a mad scientist in the best tradition of his kind. He has already managed to achieve the creation of life but only in miniature, and displays his creations—seven miniscule beings in seven bottles.

His previous attempts to enlist Dr. Frankenstein's help in his own attempts to create life having failed, Praetorius now faces Frankenstein with the Monster and forces him to help create a mate for the Monster. Frankenstein's first refusals to assist in so terrible a repetition of his work are overcome when Praetorius gets the Monster to kidnap Frankenstein's bride Elisabeth.

Praetorius' assistant steals a fresh female corpse, which, after the transplant of a new brain, is brought to life on a night when storms rage. However, as the Monster reaches out tenderly towards his freshly created 'bride' (Elsa Lanchester), his query 'friend?' is greeted with her feline screeches and a snake-like backlash of her head. The Monster realizes that he is still doomed to total loneliness and pulls a lever which, after allowing Henry Frankenstein and Elisabeth to escape, destroys the laboratory in a terrible explosion.

As for the bride herself, Miss Lanchester was built up to an extraordinary seven-foot creation with stilts and bandages, so that she had to be carried about the studio, and fed through a tube. Karloff's make-up took seven hours to prepare, so that he would be ready for shooting by 1 p.m. Changes had been made to his original make-up to take account of the fire at the end of *Frankenstein.* The flat square head of hair was burned, exposing metal clips, and his cheeks were scarred. The bride, who resembled a white-shrouded Egyptian mummy, was like the Monster, brought into being by make-up artist Pierce. Her first entrance to the ironic accompaniment of soundtrack wedding bells and music by Franz Waxman, took on the appearance of a spectre rather than the product of spare-part surgery and cosmic life forces.

Whale made *The Bride of Frankenstein* very much a personal film characterized by his quirky sense of humour, notably in the gin-sipping Praetorius of Ernest Thesiger and the too idyllic episode with the blind man, which bordered on parody. Karloff himself considered it a mistake to allow the monster to be too human, too sympathetic. The film was as much parody as horror, but while the macabre gothic touches make for humour, they also weaken the horror.

This is not to say that there should be no humour in screen horror—humour plays a most important part in the structure of horror films, especially when it is inserted deliberately to 'unwind' an audience after a climax of terror. But *The Bride of Frankenstein* succeeds more perhaps on a level of parody than on the level of pure horror achieved by *Frankenstein.*

Karloff was to don the eighteen-pound asphalt spreader's boots as the Monster for the final time in *Son of Frankenstein* (US 1938), this time insisting on portraying the creature as a cold-blooded killer rather than the speaking, almost human creature of *Bride of Frankenstein.*

This time no preamble was needed to explain the Creature's reappearance, ready for revitalization, on its marble slab in the Frankenstein secret crypt. The son of Frankenstein—Wolf—in the icy person of a very English Basil Rathbone, arrives at the village of Frankenstein to claim his inheritance, including his father's scientific papers. He finds the Monster guarded by a shepherd named Ygor

House of Frankenstein *(Universal 1944) brought together the Monster (Glenn Strange), Dracula (John Carradine), The Wolfman (Lon Chaney Jnr.) and Karloff as the mad scientist.*

—played by Lugosi—who had survived the hangman's rope, though left distorted from a broken neck.

The son meets the village inspector of police (endowed with an artificial limb to replace the arm torn from his shoulder during a previous encounter with the Monster) and is informed of the series of murders terrorizing the village. After trying to repair the Monster, Wolf revives him in full scientific glory, and allows him one brief moment of humanity when he utters a howl of animal anguish as he cradles the body of Ygor. He ends up perishing, yet again, in a pit of boiling sulphur, after kidnapping Wolf's baby son (rescued in the nick of time) and once more pulling an arm off the Police Chief (his wooden one). In two scenes the Monster shows some of the humanity that characterized him in *Bride of Frankenstein*. In one scene, Karloff finds his way to the bedroom of Wolf's son and plays with the boy, even giving him a gold watch obtained from a murdered servant! This and his genuine anguish at the death of his friend Ygor are the only traces of something other than the beast in Karloff's portrayal, his last of the Monster before handing over the eighteen-pound boots to his Universal successors.

In the next of a rapidly diminishing series (as far as quality of horror imagination went), Lon Chaney Jr took the part of the Monster in *The Ghost of Frankenstein* (US 1942). Here Chaney provided, in the words of the publicists: 'Stark Terror! Added Thrills! in a Spine-tingling Experience!' But, although Jack Pierce's make-up tried to make Chaney into another Karloff, *Ghost of Frankenstein* was the beginning of the end of the first cycle of Frankenstein films.

Chaney only gave the role brute strength with no intimations of humanity. Any pathos is provided by

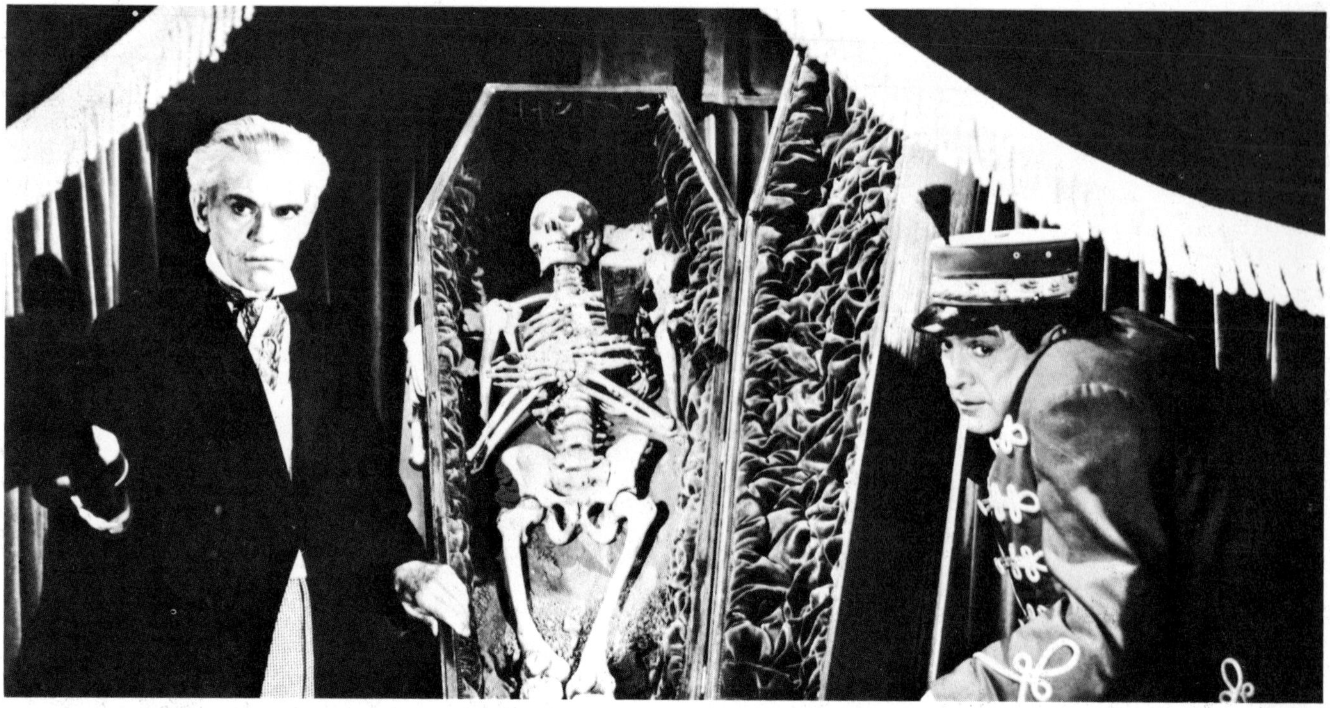

Ygor, revived by Lugosi as a hunchback, plaintively playing his recorder in the ruins of the castle, before having his brain transplanted to the Monster's skull. Revived by yet another son of Frankenstein—this time Sir Cedric Hardwicke—the Monster speaks briefly with Ygor's voice before going blind, stumbling about the laboratory, and destroying it along with Dr. Frankenstein and his assistant. Released on Friday 13th, the film was a success.

A year later in 1943, two monsters, the Frankenstein creation—played now by Lugosi—and the by-now successful Chaney werewolf met again for the monstrous fight of the century in *Frankenstein Meets The Wolf Man*. The climax of the film is in a laboratory where the Monster and the Wolf Man do battle until the patient villagers finally blow up a dam to bring the floodwaters smashing down on the fighting monsters. By now, Mary Shelley had long been forgotten, and the Monster had become synonymous with the name of its creator, Frankenstein, who didn't even appear in the film except for its title!

The Monster was to appear twice more in this cycle. In *House of Frankenstein* (1944) the cowboy actor Glenn Strange put on Karloff's boots and was coached by the great man himself. Karloff himself, in the guise of Dr. Gustav Niemann, restores the Monster to life with 'a hundred thousand megavolts' after finding him frozen in a cave along with Chaney's Wolf Man. Adding for good measure a mad scientist, a hunchback and Dracula, Universal were only hastening the end of their horror cycle. Once more, enraged villagers chased the Monster to his (temporary) death in a convenient quagmire.

The Monster returned the following year played again by Strange, in *House of Dracula* (1945), with John Carradine presiding as Dracula. This time the Monster was found entombed in the cellar of Dr. Edelman. The Doctor (Onslow Stevens), after a convenient vision which allowed use of film material of both Karloff's and Chaney's monsters, felt it incumbent upon him to revive the Monster. But, like the series, nothing could survive; the Wolfman shot Dr. Edelman and the Monster received its deserts under a falling beam when the laboratory caught fire. Nothing was changed, with the mixture of Monster, vampire, wolf man and mad scientist as before. Nothing could revive the cycle for Universal, and their Monster finally expired in 1948 with *Abbott and Costello Meet Frankenstein.*

With the exception of one or two minor films, the

ABOVE *Dr. Niemann (Boris Karloff), Dracula's skeleton and hunchback assistant (J. Carrol Naish) in* House of Frankenstein *(Universal 1944).*
ABOVE RIGHT *Checking out the Monster (Lon Chaney Jr.), the unholy trio, Frankenstein (Sir Cedric Hardwicke), Ygor (Bela Lugosi) and horror stalwart Lionel Atwill in* The Ghost of Frankenstein *(Universal 1942).*
RIGHT *Wedding day. Karloff meets his mate (Elsa Lanchester) with her creators, Colin Clive and Ernst Thesiger, in* The Bride of Frankenstein *(Universal 1935).*

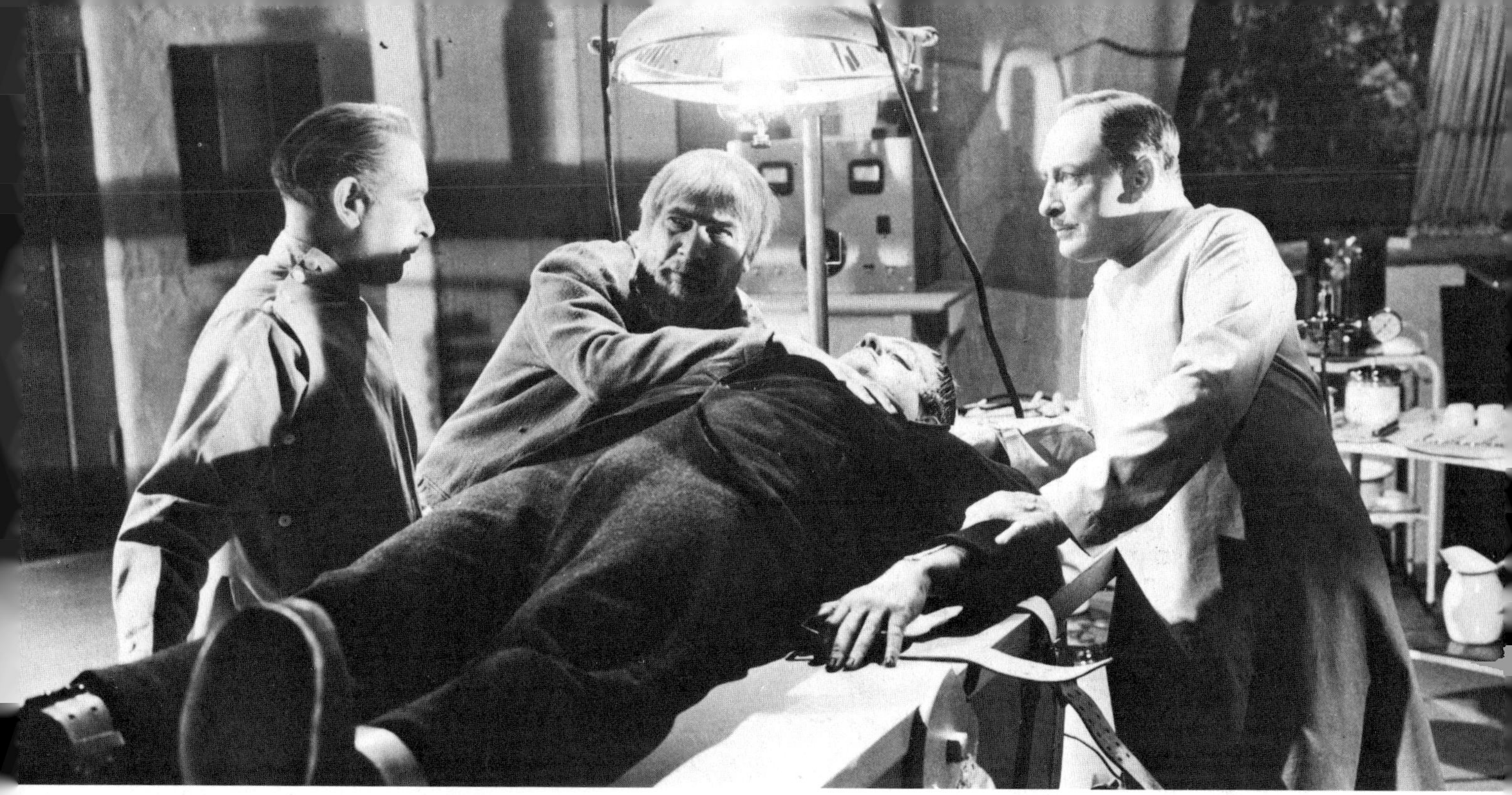

Frankenstein legend was not revived on the screen until Hammer's colour re-make of *The Curse of Frankenstein* (GB 1957). And despite cult following and the undoubted brilliance of Karloff's Monster, for many it is Hammer's colour revival which has given the screen its definitive Frankenstein, even if his monsters change from film to film. The colour Frankenstein belongs as firmly to Peter Cushing as the first Universal Monster belongs to Karloff. Cushing's incisive performance gave the Baron his own identity and helped to establish the difference between the Monster who had no name and his creator. Colour, plus literate scripts, production values and effective horror gave the new Frankenstein cycle an impetus and relevance that was to revive not only Frankenstein but the whole genre of horror.

This renaissance of the horror film was the work of one small English film company, Hammer Films, whose name was to become synonymous with screen horror for a whole new generation of cinemagoers.

After many years in the film distribution business, Hammer Films went into production after World War II. They made a number of low-budget feature films, most of them based upon the proven audience appeal of the British Broadcasting Corporation radio shows from which they were developed. Their close relationship with the B.B.C. paid off more than handsomely when Hammer made *The Quatermass Experiment* in 1955. As a television science fiction/horror serial, *The Quatermass Experiment* had disrupted the life of a nation as millions of viewers stayed riveted to their sets throughout the serial's screening. The film version was to repeat this success, but this time on an international scale, gaining Hammer's first real break into the American market. Made on a low budget, *The Quatermass Experiment* was released in the United States as *The Creeping Unknown*, there to gross over three million dollars. The new horror film era had begun and it was the start of the age of the British horror film genre.

Sir James Carreras, then head of Hammer, looked around for further ideas to capitalize upon the international success of *The Quatermass Experiment* and hit upon the concept of re-making the 'classic' horror films of the Thirties and Forties, but this time in colour. He realized that there was an entirely new audience for horror films, ready and eager for films of terror made for them and their era. And so, in 1956 Hammer revived the apparently dead Frankenstein, with their production, in vivid Eastman Colour, of *The Curse of Frankenstein*.

The script—written by Jimmy Sangster—followed Mary Shelley's story faithfully. Frankenstein once more creates a monster from parts of human cadavers taken from gallows or selected from morgues with fastidious care. Single-minded to the point of obsession, Frankenstein even murders a brilliant scientist in order to use his brain in the monster. In a struggle with his by now horrified assistant the jar containing the brain falls and is damaged by glass splinters which Frankenstein coolly removes. When the monster, swathed in bandages and drifting lifeless in the fluid of a huge glass tank, is brought to life, static electricity machines revolve and hum and electric arcs crackle as Frankenstein throws switches in a controlled crescendo of suspense. Gone are the forced perspectives and larger-than-life laboratories of the Universal films: instead, there are the glass spirals, tubes, retorts and umbilical electrical wiring of a Victorian laboratory, centering upon the monster in its giant glass tank.

For what seems like an eternity, nothing happens after Frankenstein throws the last switch and stills the final whirling static electricity generator. Then the twitch of a hand in the almost opaque liquid brings a brief moment of triumph to the scientist. The Creature possesses life, but a criminally insane life, governed by the damaged brain in its skull. The Creature, like its predecessors, escapes, kills and has half its head blown off in an almost too realistic and bloody sequence set among the greens and colours of the woods around the village. After a climactic struggle with Frankenstein on the roof of the castle, it falls through a skylight to die in a vat of acid. Frankenstein is condemned to death for the murders committed by the Creature, and the film ends with him accompanied by a priest, leaving his cell to meet death at the guillotine.

If the plot seems much 'the mixture as before', the ingredients certainly are not. The camera never flinches as Frankenstein carefully examines an eye through a magnifying glass to check its freshness and condition before paying the mortuary keeper, or unwraps a pair of hands with a connoisseur's pleasure. These details, which could have become in the hands of lesser actors and directors merely gratuitously unpleasant, become, under Terence Fisher's skilled and unobtrusive direction and Cushing's cool, incisive playing of Frankenstein, integral to the film. *The Curse of Frankenstein* was horror for its time, played seriously by all its actors, written with sensibility and directed with flair. There was no hint of small budgets or rushed production—the sets were handsomely mounted, the film beautifully photographed and made, with horrors, both explicit and implicit, brilliantly integrated. The style was set for horror films from then on, up to Hammer's 1973 *Frankenstein and the Monster from Hell.*

While Sangster's script had been able to base itself upon the original story, the Monster make-up created for Karloff by Jack Pierce in 1931 was copyright, and so Phil Leakey was forced to re-think the 'creature' and its appearance, much as Pierce had had to do. Even more than Pierce, Phil Leakey appreciated that his 'creature' would be very much the result of 'real' surgery involving 'real' human tissue and organs, and it would have the added advantages of colour (particularly in the sequence when half the creature's head is shot off in a welter of Eastman Colour blood). For the purists, his creature did not have the power and impact of the Karloff monster. Nonetheless, in the context of *The Curse of Frankenstein*, the creature worked—there was no laughter in the wrong places, and the creature evoked horror for the audiences of that time.

The actor who was selected to play the creature was Christopher Lee, 6 foot 5 inches tall. 'They wanted a tall man for obvious reasons, and because of the dominance and power of the character. They also,' says Lee, 'wanted somebody who could act without words, something made even more difficult because of the make-up which left me with only one eye as the other one was blind.'

Like Karloff before him, Lee suffered in portraying the creature, but the result was well worth it. Although, unlike Karloff, Lee has never again played the Frankenstein monster, it was this part which launched him firmly into a starring career in horror films, a role that was to be clinched when he played *Dracula*, which was released in 1958.

The Curse of Frankenstein marked the start of the long sequence of horror films starring Cushing and Lee together. In fact, they had been in the same film once before. That film was Laurence Olivier's *Hamlet*! Peter Cushing had already established himself as a household name as an actor on television before playing the part of Baron Victor Frankenstein. He had started in repertory at the Connaught Theatre in Worthing before borrowing some money from his father to go to America where he landed a minor part almost immediately in the film *The Man in The Iron Mask* with Louis Hayward. The director, prophetically, was James Whale who had directed *Frankenstein* and *The Bride of Frankenstein.*

Hammer monster Christopher Lee in Phil Leakey's new make-up in The Curse of Frankenstein *(Hammer 1957).*

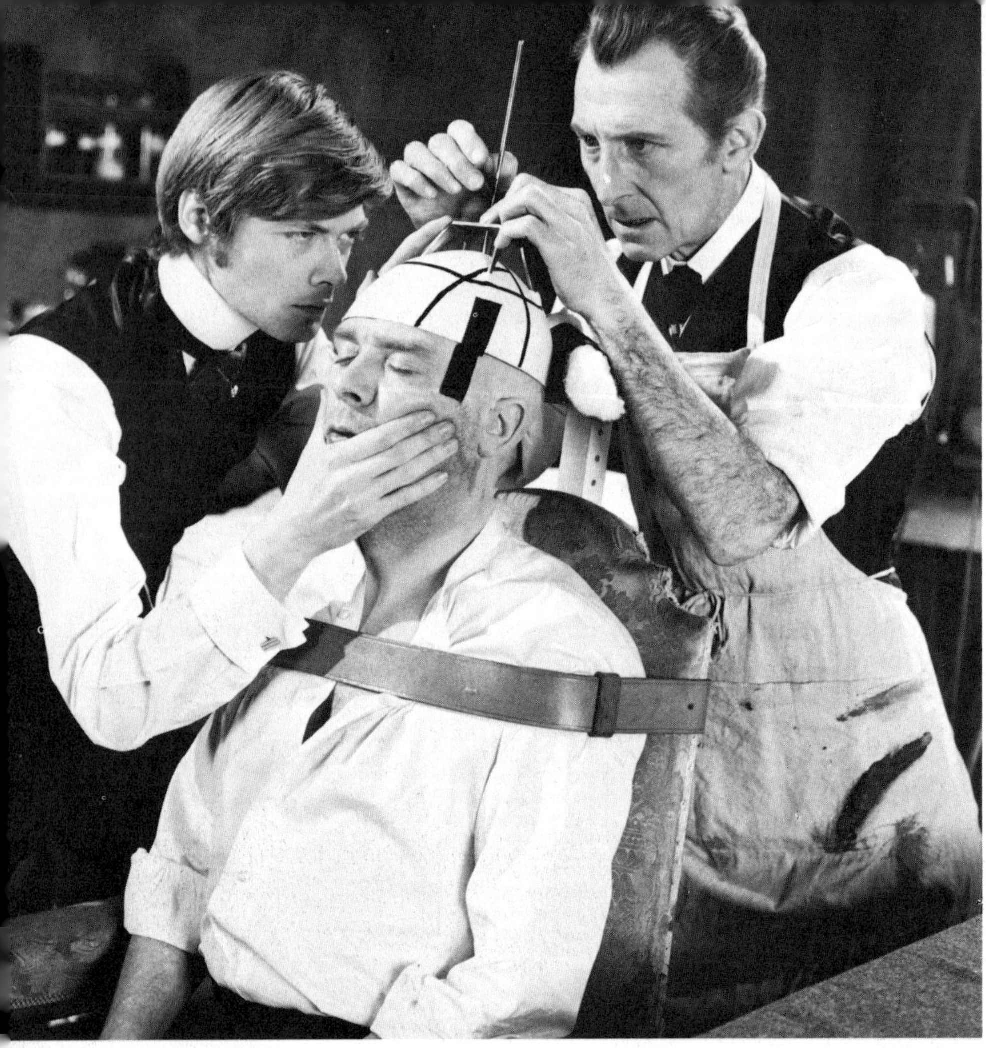

Frankenstein Hammer-style. The greatest Baron of them all, Peter Cushing is seen here with:
LEFT *assistant Simon Ward and victim Freddie Jones in* Frankenstein Must Be Destroyed! *(Hammer 1969);*
BELOW *fellow experimenter Sandor Eles in* The Evil of Frankenstein *(Hammer 1964);*
RIGHT *helper Thorley Walters in Terry Fisher's* Frankenstein Created Woman *(Hammer 1967). The bisexually malevolent result was played by Susan Denberg* (below right).

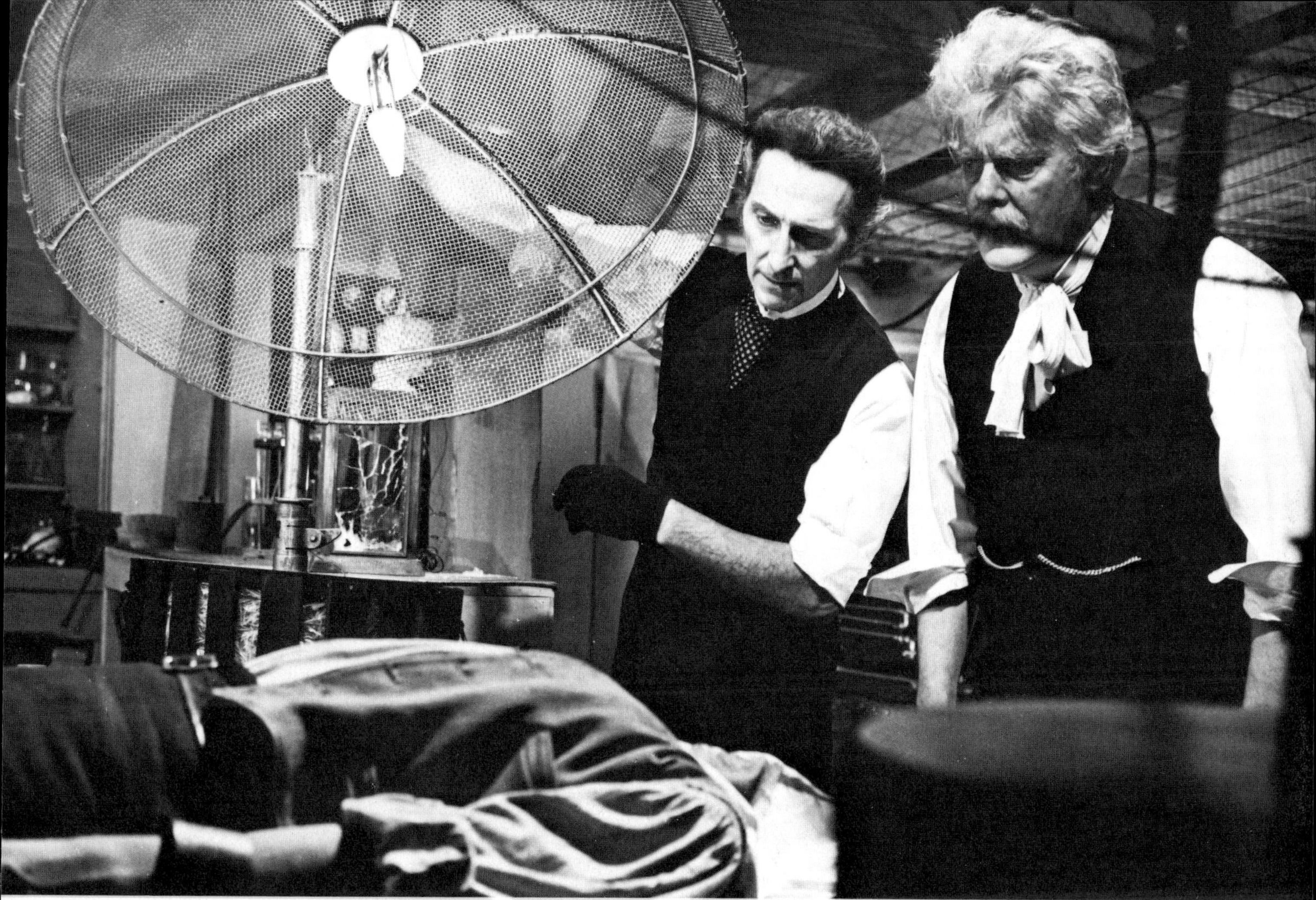

After wartime service with E.N.S.A., Cushing began to work in the theatre and toured overseas with the Old Vic Company. But it was television that was to make him a star: between 1951 and 1956, he appeared in over twenty major television plays, including *Home at Seven*, *Gaslight*, *The Winslow Boy* and an award-winning performance as Winston Smith in the television version of George Orwell's horrifying novel *1984*.

Then Peter Cushing accepted the Hammer film role of Victor Frankenstein, a part which he has made exclusively his, in addition to a gallery of other equally compelling and powerful horror roles.

Cushing's performance as Frankenstein was played completely seriously, almost clinically, so that nothing became laughable and scenes which had the potential to nauseate—his examination of the dissected eye through a magnifying glass, the hacking and cutting necessary to assemble his creature—were never revolting but became logical extensions of his actions and ambitions. Cushing had read Mary Shelley's novel before playing the role, but his Frankenstein was more than just the sum of the original book and Sangster's script. His acting developed the character so that in the following series of Frankenstein films it was the Baron who was 'revived' and became the centre of each film, rather than the 'monster'. Cushing has described Frankenstein as 'brilliant, a brilliant surgeon with fantastic ideas, but unfortunately something always does go wrong with the brain of the unfortunate creatures he manages to make.'

The film contained one laugh, injected into the film to release the audience's tension after a climax, so that the film could build up again to another even more powerful climax. Baron Frankenstein becomes tired of importuning a servant girl whom he had once promised to marry. He gets her down to the cell in which the creature is held captive. He locks her in the cell with the creature and, as it lumbers towards the now screaming girl to kill her, we see the Baron standing quizzically outside the cell, apparently oblivious to the girl's horrifying screams.

Then there comes an abrupt cut to a most domestic breakfast scene, with Frankenstein and his fiancée (Hazel Court) together at the sunlit table. Frankenstein finishes buttering a piece of toast and asks politely 'Pass the marmalade!' The deliberate incongruity of this scene and the horror of the girl's death before it sets the audience laughing.

The Curse of Frankenstein was directed by Terence Fisher who had already directed a number of films for Hammer. Asked if he would like to see Whale's original *Frankenstein* Fisher declined. This approach was to pay dividends. Gone was the Germanic influence in the sets, and the outrageous overacting that had marred sequences in the first films. With colour and superb production values,

RIGHT *Rank Film Distributors' poster for* The Evil of Frankenstein *(Hammer 1964).*
BELOW *Ralph Bates and Dave Prowse in* Horror of Frankenstein *(Hammer 1970).*

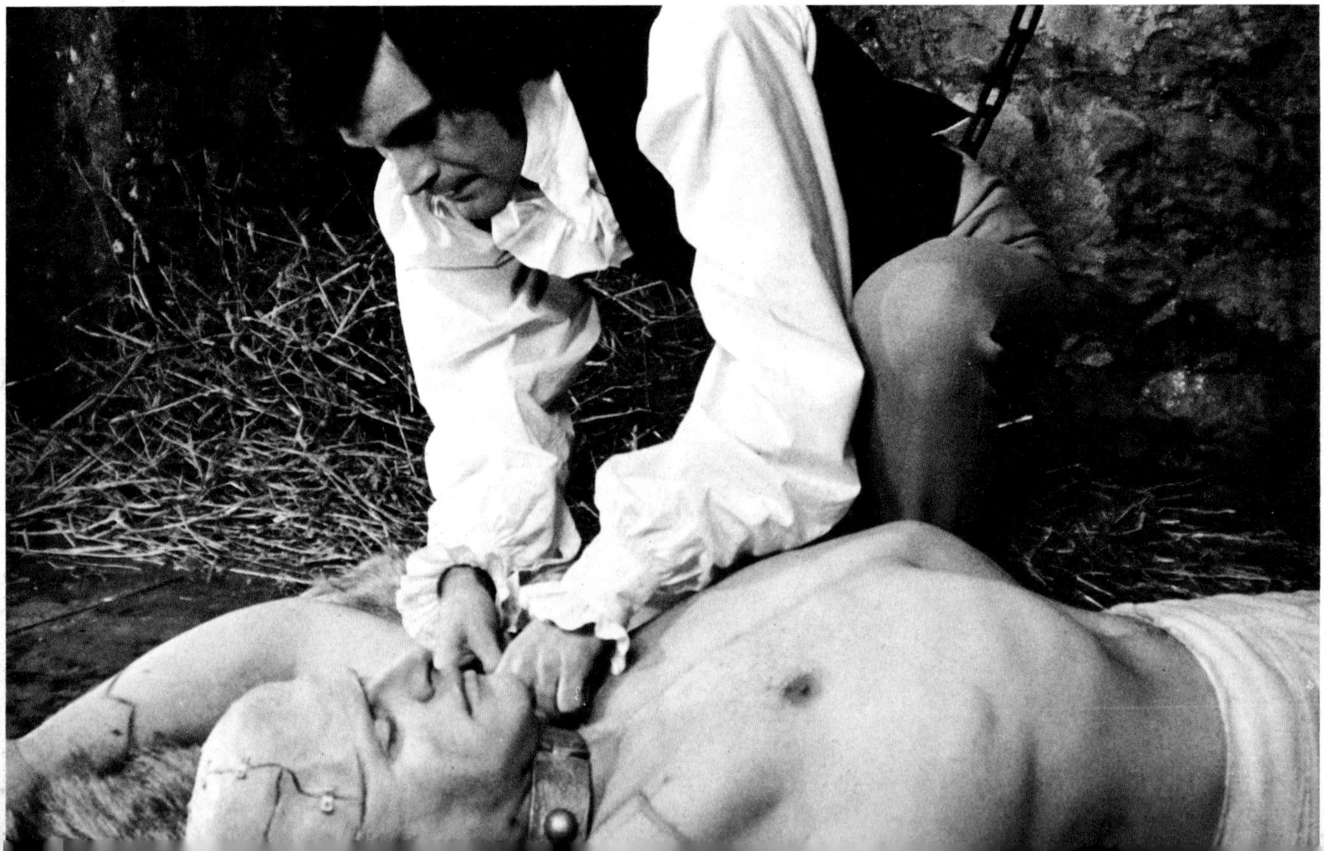

SHOCK... SHOCK...
PETER CUSHING
THE EVIL OF FRANKENSTEIN
CERT X ADULTS ONLY
EASTMAN COLOUR
ALSO STARRING
PETER WOODTHORPE DUNCAN LAMONT WITH SANDOR ELES
Story and Screenplay by JOHN ELDER
Produced by ANTHONY HINDS
Directed by FREDDIE FRANCIS
A HAMMER FILM PRODUCTION FOR UNIVERSAL-INTERNATIONAL

and a use of lenses that made small sets seem infinitely larger, Fisher made as personal a film as the original, but without any obtrusive 'tricks' to distract the audience from the drama they were watching. 'You have to make the audience believe in the people, the characters that you have on the screen in a situation, for at least an hour and a half'. There has to be that vital suspension of disbelief.

It was not until the film was half made that Fisher began to realize that with *The Curse of Frankenstein*, Hammer had 'got something in their pocket which was tremendous'. This was an understatement from the man who directed the film that grossed over seven million dollars and joined the pantheon of horror films. To Fisher, the horror must be integral to the development of the film, and not something grafted on for additional and unmotivated unpleasantness. He does not, however, subscribe to the view that horror should always be implied rather than seen. 'I know it's popular and fashionable to say the unseen is the most scaring—I don't believe this,' says Fisher. 'I think the most scaring thing I can think of was in the first Frankenstein, the first movement of the monster in the tank coming to life—and that was just a twitch of a hand . . .'

Cushing, saved from the guillotine at the end of *The Curse of Frankenstein* by the substitution of the priest who was accompanying him to his death, returned in 1958 in *The Revenge of Frankenstein.* Once again Fisher directed in colour, and Cushing, in the disguise of Dr. Stein, continued his experiments in the creation of life to produce a 'handsome' monster (Michael Gwynne) whose brain, as usual, let him down so that he grew progressively more evil after being damaged in a fight, finally to turn cannibal! The traditional mob pursued 'Dr. Stein' who escaped, however, to turn up with a Harley Street practice under the new name of Professor Franck, ready for his next film incarnation!

In 1964, *The Evil of Frankenstein*—Hammer's 88th film, and the 50th to be produced for the Company by Anthony Hinds—brought Cushing back once again. Baron Frankenstein, once more fleeing from irate villagers, escapes to discover, frozen in ice and ready for thawing, the monstrous result of one of his previous experiments. With the help of a hypnotist, Cushing revives his monster, in appearance far nearer the Karloff creation, and played by a famous New Zealand wrestler, Kiwi Kingston. The new monster is soon terrorizing the neighbourhood with murders. Meanwhile the Baron has to fight for control of the creature with the hypnotist, and, having apparently won the battle for possession, both he and his monster come to a violent and spectacular end in a flaming holocaust.

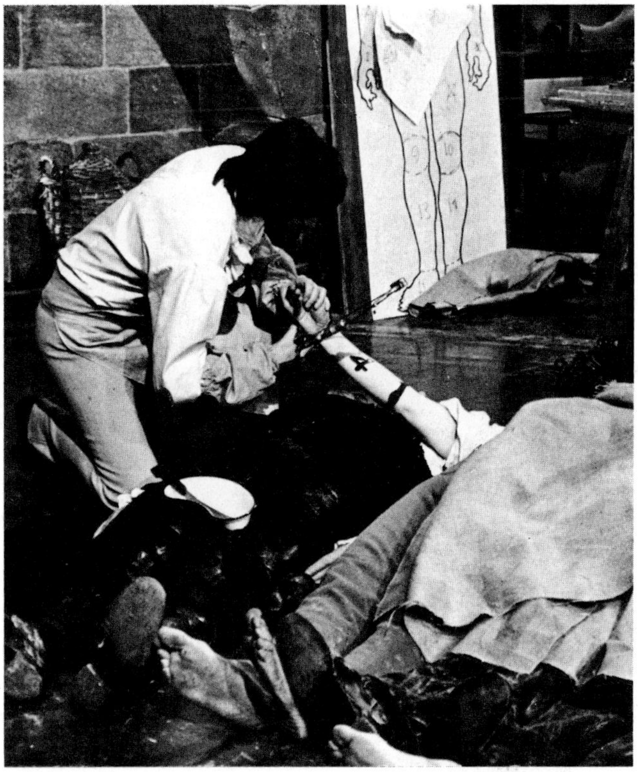

PRECEDING PAGES *Leonard Whiting and David McCallum in a scene from* Frankenstein, The True Story *(Universal 1974).*
LEFT *In the same film, James Mason as Dr. Polidori forces Leonard Whiting to assist him in creating Prima.*
ABOVE *Ralph Bates builds a monster by numbers in Jimmy Sangster's* Horror of Frankenstein *(Hammer 1970).*

The flames may well have been too much for Mr. Kingston who, after brief stardom, presumably returned to the more prosaic life of the all-in wrestling ring, but the Baron returned to Bray Studios where, in 1967, *Frankenstein Created Woman.*

This creation was not as horrifying as had been the *Bride of Frankenstein*, at least, not to look at. The woman in question was the actress Susan Denberg, a new arrival on the horror scene. In *Frankenstein Created Woman* Peter Cushing ensured that her beauty was only skin deep, reviving her from death by drowning by giving her the soul of a man—Hans, who has been guillotined earlier in the film. Christina (Susan Denberg) now beautiful but bisexual, uses her body to lure to their deaths the three youths for whose crime Hans was beheaded. She manages to kill all three before throwing herself from a cliff to drown once more in a pounding torrent of water. Once again, the Baron had failed. But was he downhearted? No!

Dave Prowse, the Monster, lays eyes on the delightful Kate O'Mara in Horror of Frankenstein *(Hammer 1970).*

He returned in 1969 in *Frankenstein Must Be Destroyed.* Terence Fisher directed the complex story of Cushing's attempts at brain transplant surgery, aided by his able helper Simon ('Young Winston') Ward. For a while, things seem to go well, with Professor Richter (Freddie Jones) bearing the transplanted brain of Doctor Brandt, apparently one of the Baron's successes. Inevitably, though, things go from bad to disastrous until, in a blazing house, Richter/Brandt and Frankenstein fight to the death.

Cushing unfortunately did not appear in the next Frankenstein film from Hammer, and the film suffered accordingly from the lack of his always believable and superbly acted Frankenstein. *Horror of Frankenstein* (1970) starred Ralph Bates as Victor Frankenstein, a descendant of the original Baron who appeared to be more interested in sex than more unorthodox methods of creating life. Jimmy Sangster, who had written the first *Curse of Frankenstein,* wrote, produced and directed what was a black comedy remake of the first of the Hammer Frankenstein pictures. Sangster was able to extract a certain amount of sick humour from the situations, but the Monster, played by David Prowse, was no more than a convenient strong-arm brute to rid Victor Frankenstein of unwanted friends and acquaintances. Nothing so much became this monster's 'life' as its leaving it, with a last view of giant boots bobbing on the surface of a vat of acid.

To the delight of all those aficionados of the horror film, 1973 saw the reunion of Cushing as Baron Frankenstein and Director Terence Fisher in the latest of the continuing story of the Baron in *Frankenstein and the Monster From Hell.* The sixth film in which Cushing has made the part of Frankenstein very much his own finds him living as the asylum doctor at Carlsbad under the name of Dr. Victor. Frankenstein is engaged in his eternal quest

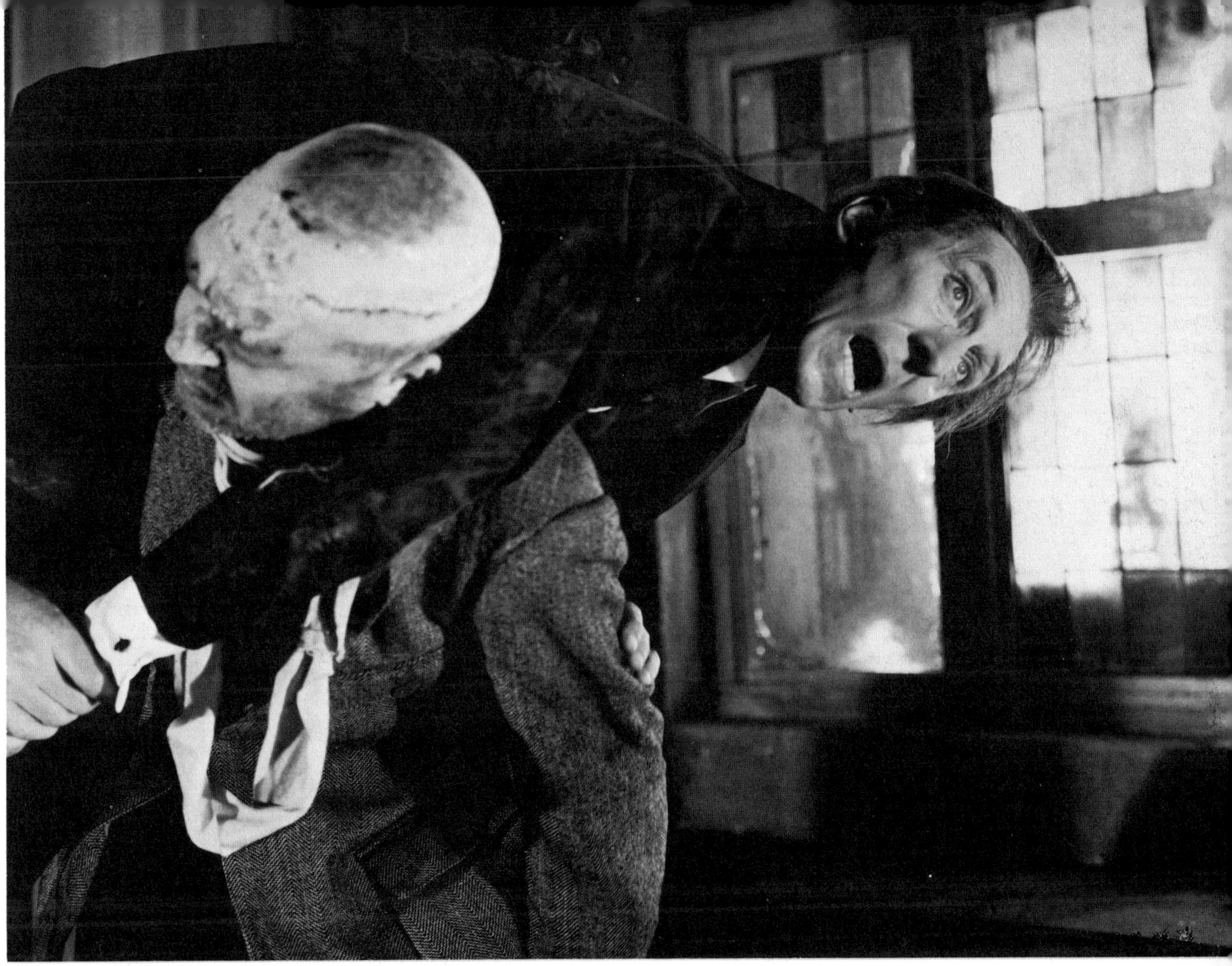

Creature Freddie Jones and creator Peter Cushing fight to the death in Frankenstein Must Be Destroyed! *(Hammer 1969).*

for the creation of life, using human organs and limbs from dead inmates of the asylum. Dr. Victor is recognized by one of his admirers who discovers the experiments on which Cushing is engaged and joins in assisting him. Once more things go wrong and the monster, played again by David Prowse, is killed in the climactic battle with a crowd of rioting lunatics.

With Cushing back firmly in the character of Baron Frankenstein, the second cinematic phase of the Mary Shelley creation continues, with Cushing and Hammer supplying the heartbeat of the Frankenstein revival. But other films on the theme have appeared since *The Curse of Frankenstein* (1956). *I was a Teenage Frankenstein* (US 1957) was as ludicrous as its title and earned for it the somewhat dubious distinction of being named one of the worst horror films ever made. Put together from various bits of teenage corpses by mad scientist Whit Bissell who at that time represented the American branch of the Frankenstein family, the resulting monster played by Gary Conway ended up with a face thrown together in a fit of amnesia, a superb physique and all the normal appetites and interests of the typical American teenager of the time. With such gems of dialogue as 'Answer me, you have a civil tongue in your head. I know, I sewed it in there' from Whit Bissell, the film deserves its place as a footnote in the story of Frankenstein! Needless to say, it also made a fortune at the box office.

The year 1957 also saw Karloff's last appearance in a Frankenstein film, *Frankenstein 1970*, in which he played the creator for the first time, a fully paid-up member of the Frankenstein clan. Karloff was Victor Frankenstein, disfigured by Nazi tortures in both mind and body. In using atomic power to try to bring back to life the monster created by his 18th-century ancestor, both Karloff and the creature are destroyed by radioactive steam.

In 1956, wholeheartedly but ineptly, Japan con-

ABOVE *The Monster gets to grips with Kate O'Mara in* Horror of Frankenstein *(Hammer 1970).*
BELOW *Atomically created giant name-dropper goes to war in* Frankenstein Conquers the World *(Toho 1965).*
RIGHT *A benign Peter Cushing in clerical garb as Dr. Blyss, alias Capt. Clegg, in* Night Creatures *(Hammer-Major 1962).*

tributed the film *Frankenstein Conquers The World*, in which the living heart of the Frankenstein monster, shipped to Hiroshima near the end of World War II, is subjected to radiation from the atom bomb dropped on the city, and grows into a wild boy called Frankenstein. Growing at a startling rate, this monster is held responsible for the misdeeds of a huge reptile, Baragon, released by an earthquake from its hibernation since prehistoric times. The film ends in the middle of an earthquake. Baragon is destroyed and the monster is buried by the earthquake. It is hardly surprising that the Baron did not bother to travel to Japan on this occasion, leaving the creature's revival to the unselective power of the atom bomb.

The American *Duel of the Space Monsters*, originally titled *Frankenstein Meets the Space Monster*, was an attempt to use the name to revive an already moribund film. The 'monster' turned out to be nothing more than an 'astrorobot' with half its head blown off to display what looked alarmingly like the entrails of an alarm clock and the film was no more than a piece of science fiction hokum. If the Baron had ever been in a grave long enough, he would have been spinning in it after this film!

Universal used a variation of their original make-up on Herman Munster (Fred Gwynne) in *Munster Go Home* (US 1966), a film version of the television series *The Munster Family*. The monster, played for laughs, had nothing but the make-up to commend him, and the film did not even have the lethal powers once possessed by the Studio's prime horror executioners, Abbott and Costello.

Finally, just to show that Frankenstein was able to keep up with current trends, Victor Frankenstein (Robin Ward), expelled from university in Transylvania, came to Canada to continue experimentation under the tutelage of Professor Preston (Sean Sullivan). As usual, Frankenstein is expelled, this time unjustly accused of possessing marijuana! Bent on revenge, he takes over the mind of a karate-expert friend and embarks on a series of revenge murders. Ultimately the friend regains control and kills Frankenstein, who falls over a bannister, and while the karate expert and Frankenstein's girlfriend watch in horror, his skin begins to split open. *Frankenstein on Campus* (Canada 1969) cashed in on the name so carefully and brilliantly built up by Cushing, without adding anything to the cycle.

Frankenstein now lives on in the more than capable hands of Peter Cushing and in the monster that Karloff made. He will undoubtedly survive long after his campus capers, teenage, duels and monster fights have been forgotten!

Leonard Whiting as Dr. Frankenstein (left) *assembles his components to make the initially handsome creature, Michael Sarrazin* (right) *in* Frankenstein, The True Story *(Universal 1974).*
BELOW *Peter Cushing and Simon Ward open the skull of George Pravda in* Frankenstein Must Be Destroyed! *(Hammer 1969).*

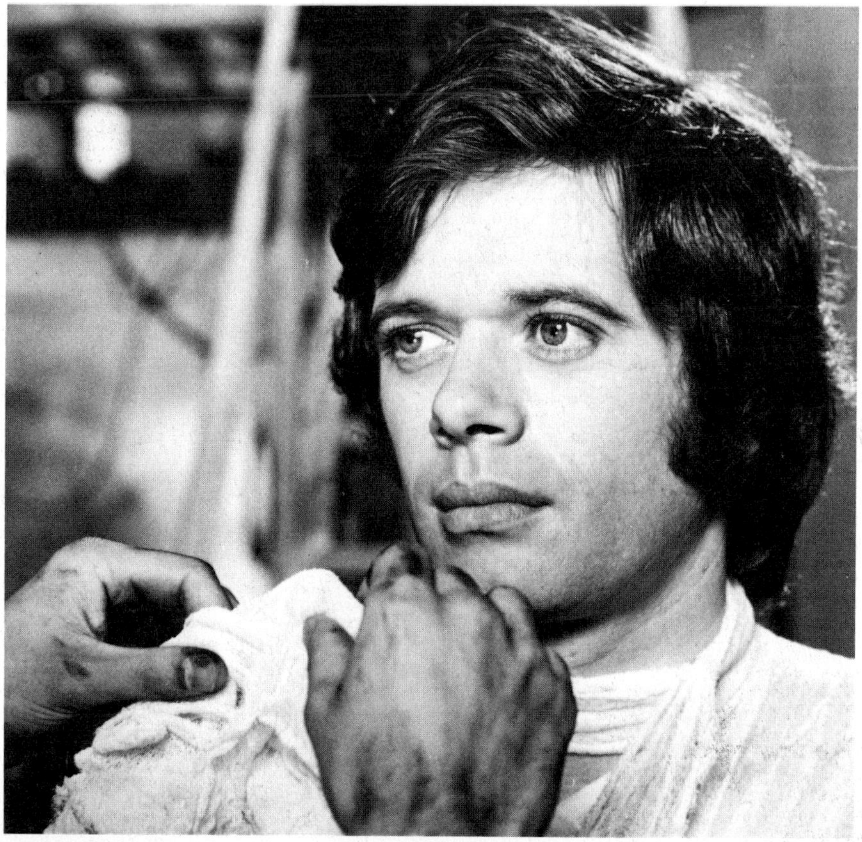

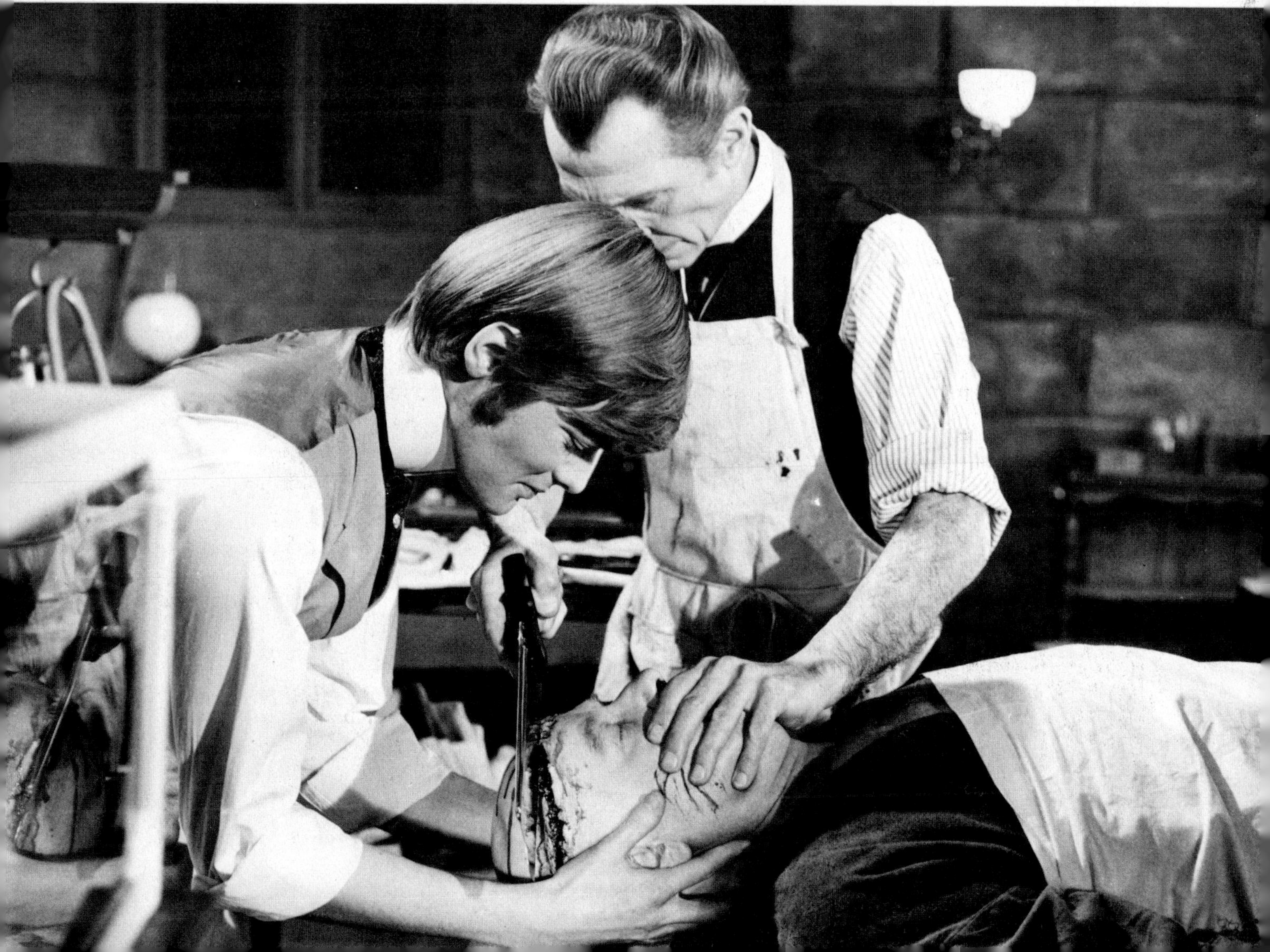

THE COUNT

"Whoever plays Dracula makes the picture. I was fortunate enough to give an interpretation of a character which was personal, purely personal, one of my own, and which paid off." Christopher Lee

COUNT DRACULA, certainly the most attractive and virile of all screen monsters, has enjoyed a cinema existence almost as long as that of his titled friend, Baron Frankenstein. Like Frankenstein, Dracula and his fellow vampires show little sign of flagging despite a screen life dating from trick films in 1896 up to *The Satanic Rites of Dracula* (GB 1973).

Apart from the physically repulsive habits of the genuine vampire bat, the legend of Dracula precedes Bram Stoker's famous novel *Dracula* published in 1897. Indeed, two earlier major novels featured the vampire legend, and were, strangely, written by two of the men who had been with Mary Shelley when she conceived Frankenstein. Lord Byron published *Giaour* in 1813 and Dr. John Polidori followed this with *The Vampyre* in 1819. Probably none of these writers knew, however, of the real-life monster who gave his name to the screen monster. In the latter years of the 15th century lived Prince Vlad V of Wallachia, known as Vlad the Impaler. Among other unpleasant deeds, he was credited with the impaling of 23,000 Turkish prisoners and was, as Lee says '. . . a real monster.' From his father, an equally unpleasant gentleman called Dracul, meaning the Devil, he took his name 'Dracula', literally the 'Son of the Devil'.

Certainly in the cinema, Dracula has lived up to his historical antecedents. His first major appearance was in F. W. Murnau's *Nosferatu: Eine Symphonie des Grauens* made in Germany in 1921. Murnau had already filmed a version of Robert

Two faces of Bela Lugosi as Count Dracula; in the title role (left) *in* Dracula *(Universal 1931), and in a posed publicity still near the end of his career* (right).

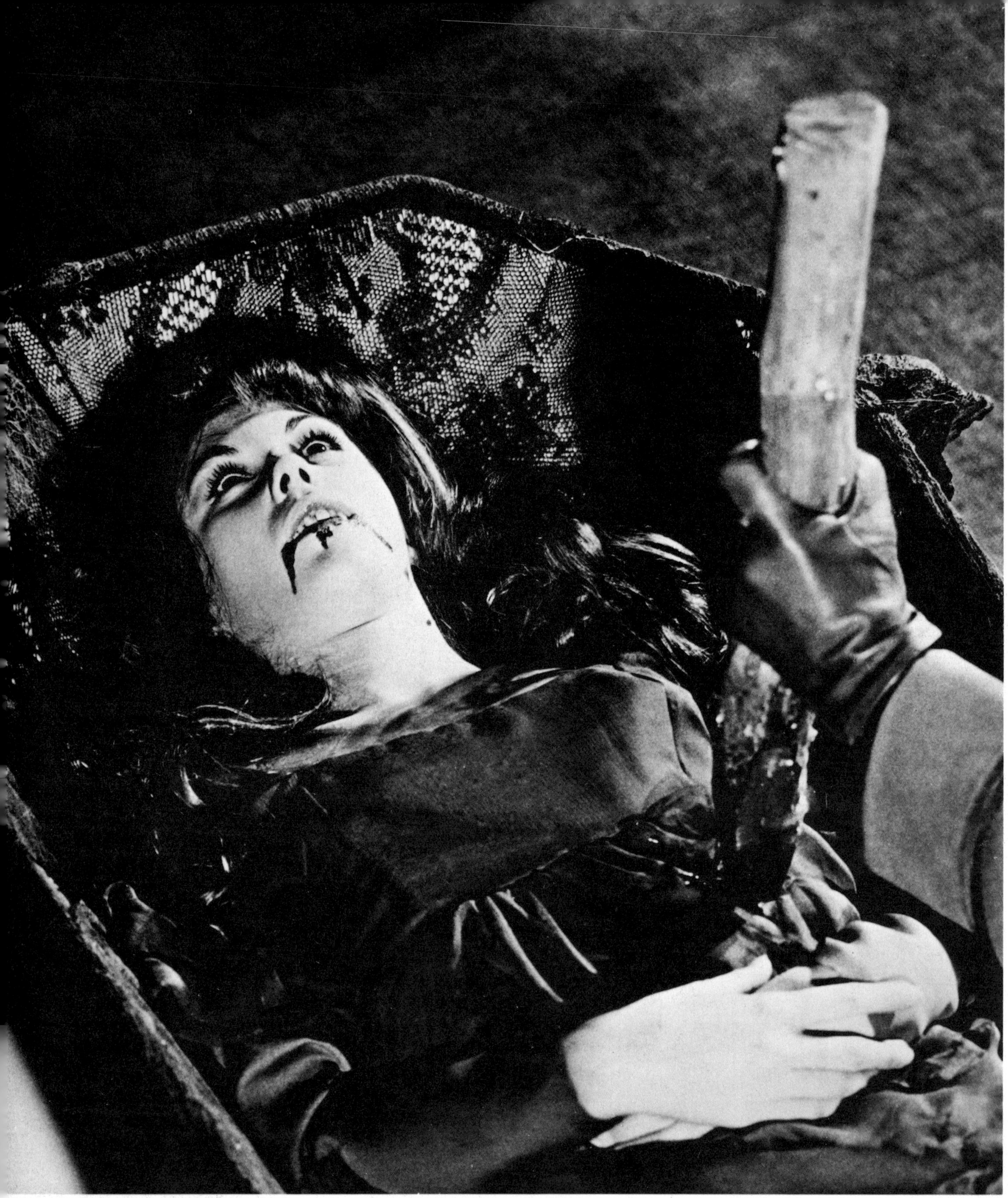

ABOVE *The vampire meets nemesis in the traditional manner in* Count Dracula *(Fenix/Corona/Filmar/Towers 1970).*
ABOVE RIGHT *Max Schreck as Count Orloff disintegrates in the sunlight in Murnau's* Nosferatu *(Prana 1922).*
RIGHT *'I am Dracula . . . I bid you welcome!' Transylvanian hospitality from Bela Lugosi to Dwight Frye in* Dracula *(Universal 1931).*

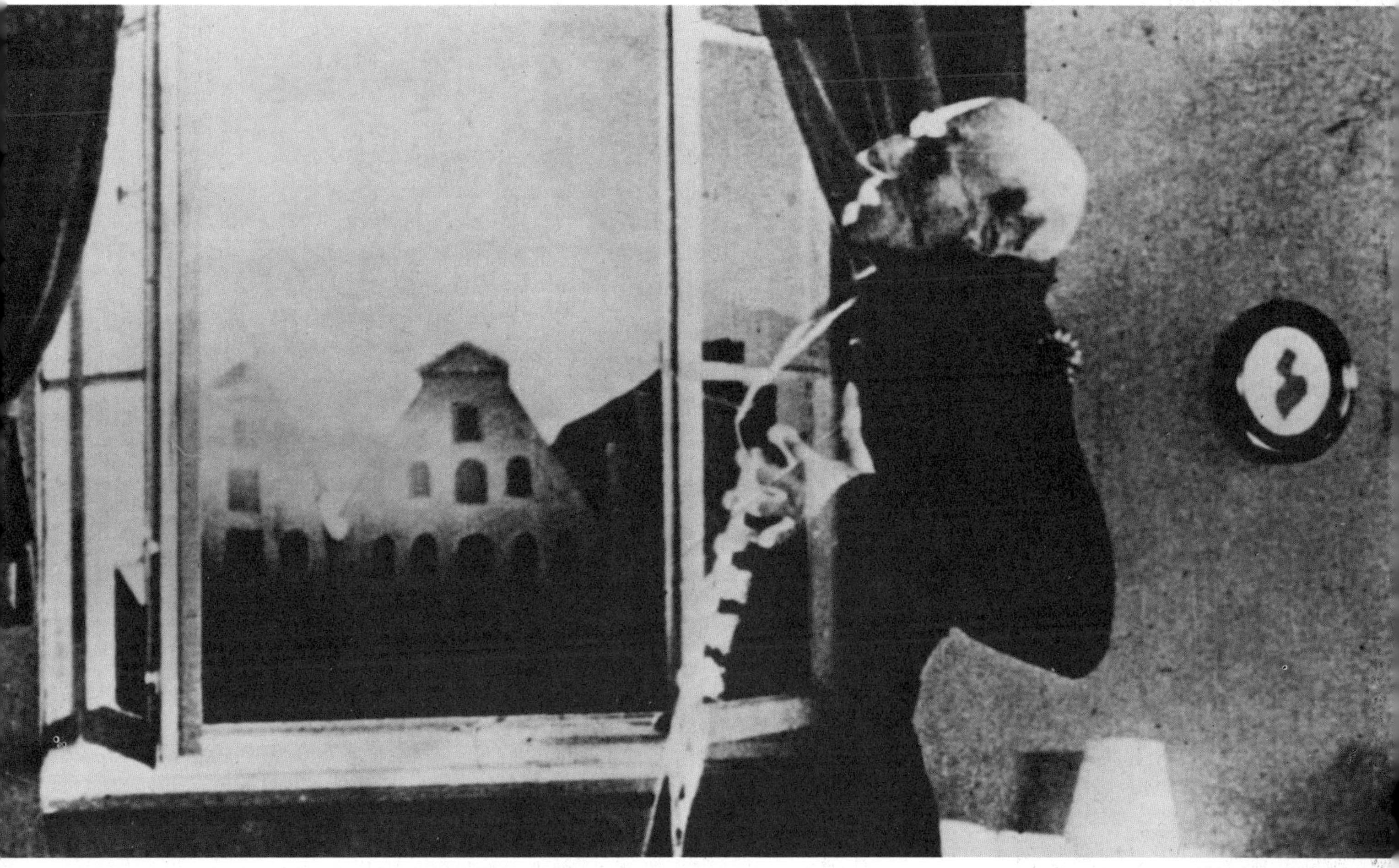

Louis Stevenson's *Dr. Jekyll and Mr. Hyde*, adapting it and changing its title to *Der Januskopf* so as to avoid royalty payments. Similarly he had not bothered to get permission to use either Stoker's story line or title, and so Murnau's adaptor, Henrik Galeen, changed the names of the characters and its settings. Nevertheless, Stoker's widow won a court case against the film's makers obtaining an order for the destruction of all prints of the film. Film 'pirates', however, usually see to it that such orders are never fully carried out, and prints of *Nosferatu* have survived, like Dracula, for posterity.

In Galeen's adaptation, the hero Jonathan Harker becomes 'Hutter' and starts the film in a standard horror opening sequence with a wild coach ride through the mist-shrouded forests of Transylvania to the castle of Graf Orlok, as Dracula is now named. Played by Max Schreck, Orlok is a truly revolting creation with sunken eyes set in skull-like features with a hairless pate, a distorted body and talons longer than his hands. He was easily the most vile of all screen vampires, without any of the potent magnetism that Lugosi and Lee were to bring to the part. Orlok was a creature of unredeemed evil.

Although Hutter was spared the fangs of his hungry host (apparently through some form of telepathy with Hutter's wife, miles away in Bremen, who wakes screaming when Orlok bends over her sleeping husband thus putting the vampire off his intended meal), most of the film's remaining players were not so lucky. After missing his chance at Hutter, Orlok sails on the ship *Empusa* for Bremen and on board seizes his opportunities with both jaws. As the ship sails into Bremen it is crewed only by the dead with the corpse of its captain lashed to the wheel. Bremen suffers a blood feast until Orlok, enticed by Hutter's wife Ellen into an embrace, disintegrates in a puff of smoke when the sunlight, into which he has been lured, strikes him. Novelist André Gide found the film heavy-handed, absurd and unimaginative and certainly time has not been kind to it. What the film did achieve was the creation of the first, and certainly most repulsive, screen vampire.

The now famous 1931 version of Dracula *(Universal), directed by Tod Browning. The infamous Count is seen at home* (below), *preparing to dine* (right).

Lon Chaney Snr. was the next film vampire in *London After Midnight* (US 1927). But the film, known as *The Hypnotist* in Britain, was basically a cheat, lacking the courage of its pretensions. While Chaney scuttles around the Hollywood London with the apparent semblance and inclinations of the vampire, particularly in his hideously grotesque make-up, he turns out to be a fake, shedding his disguise, fangs and all, to reveal himself as Inspector Burke of Scotland Yard, whose vampire antics have been a hoax to trap a killer. In effect, the audience is hoaxed. True they had Chaney in one of his most convincing portrayals, with make-up even more painful to use than that for the monster devised for the silent *Phantom of the Opera*: he created his twisted vampire with thin wires to make his eyes stand out, and teeth which made it impossible for him to speak. But, the dénouement ruined the vampire legend as far as the film was concerned.

The film's director, Tod Browning rationalized the trick ending, saying '. . . The audience is not asked to believe the horrible impossible, but the horrible possible, and plausibility increased, rather than lessened, the thrills and chills.' But when he came to make *Dracula* for Universal in 1931 Browning was able to put aside such reservations about cinema audience credulity. As a result, *Dracula* made a star of Bela Lugosi, star of the Broadway stage version, and gave Universal their first classic screen monster.

Although nearly fifty when he achieved stardom, Lugosi exuded a middle-European magnetism which, allied with his aura of courteous and epicene menace, slicked-down patent-leather hair, and an accent that reeked of Transylvania, made him into Dracula. Audiences everywhere accepted him, immaculate in evening dress and cloak, staring at them hypnotically through the swirling mists, and

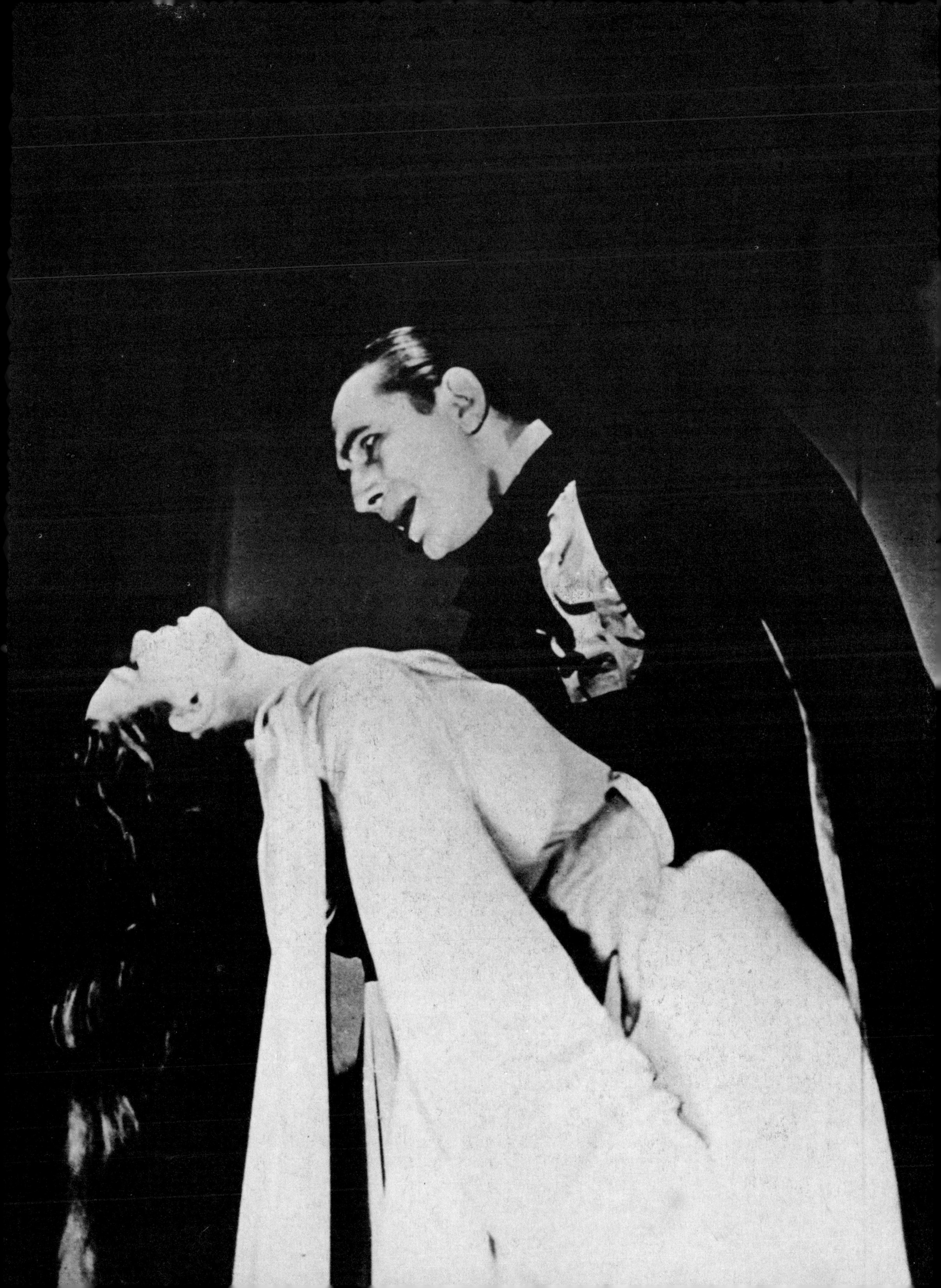

ABOVE *The screen's greatest Count Dracula, Christopher Lee, perishes in* The Satanic Rites of Dracula *(Hammer 1973)*.
TOP LEFT *Lee in* Dracula, Prince of Darkness *(Hammer-Seven Arts 1965)*.
TOP RIGHT *Patrick Troughton is attacked in* The Scars of Dracula *(Hammer/EMI 1970)*.
RIGHT *William Marshall gets his teeth into a victim in* Blacula *(AIP 1972)*.
FAR RIGHT *The end of an unwilling vampire (Jon Pertwee) in Peter Duffell's* The House That Dripped Blood *(Amicus 1970)*.

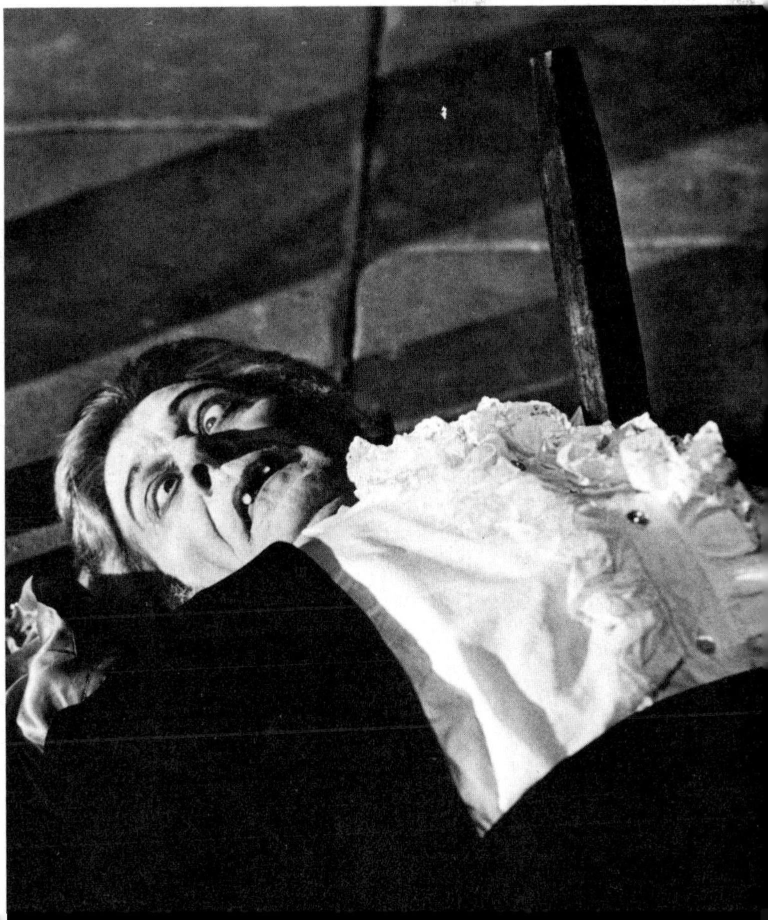

immortalizing the vampire with his opening words: 'I am Count Dracula . . . I bid you welcome.'

Indeed he made Renfield (Dwight Frye) most welcome when, after the obligatory coach ride through the oppressive wastes of the Transylvanian countryside, Renfield enters the crumbling Gothic ruins of Castle Dracula. Superbly photographed in black and white by Karl Freund, the castle is genuinely eerie, an immense vastness of huge mouldering staircases, great empty fireplaces, rat-infested coffins, the silent gliding of the three ghostly wives of Dracula, and everywhere, great cobwebs that seem to be holding the whole edifice together.

In such a setting it is hardly surprising that in a short while Count Dracula has Renfield enslaved, the latter willingly entering into the spirit of things by starting with the eating of flies, graduating to spiders, as part of his journey towards the ultimate delights of vampirism!

The film loses its initial impact, however, when the action switches to England where Renfield takes his master, comfortable in his coffin, by sea to Whitby. By the time the *Vesta* reaches its destination, Renfield is the last person alive on board! The Count moves to Carfax Abbey, a pleasant reminder of his own battlements in Transylvania, and soon begins to yearn for the jugular vein of his neighbour's daughter Mina. He enters her bedroom as a flapping bat, to materialize over the sleeping girl. Here he meets nemesis in the form of the suitably armed and knowledgeable Van Helsing (Edward Van Sloan) who forces Dracula off-screen with wolfbane, there to drive a stake through his heart, unseen. All that was left for Lugosi was a rather feeble off-screen groan, so that the film missed out on the horror which could so well have been made more explicit. *Dracula* promised more horror than it delivered and that may be one reason for its dated look today. The direction is uninspired, the delivery of lines still stagey, but Lugosi's performance saves it. He *is* Dracula, evil to the very end, with a sexual magnetism that brought him, at the height of his popularity, as much fan mail as any romantic film star.

In 1935, after the success of *Dracula* had set in motion a spate of vampire films, Metro-Goldwyn-Mayer allowed Tod Browning to make *Mark of the Vampire* with Lugosi and Lionel Barrymore, the former playing the 'vampire' while Barrymore acted the part of the detective, and the setting moved to Czechoslovakia. The 'vampirism' in the film was explained away this time as the activities of vaudeville performers involved in the solving of

ABOVE *Evelyn Ankers and mentor see the bat in* Son of Dracula *(Universal 1943).*
Dracula incarnate (right) *and the death of Dracula* (overleaf); *two scenes from* The Satanic Rites of Dracula *(Hammer 1973), starring Christopher Lee.*

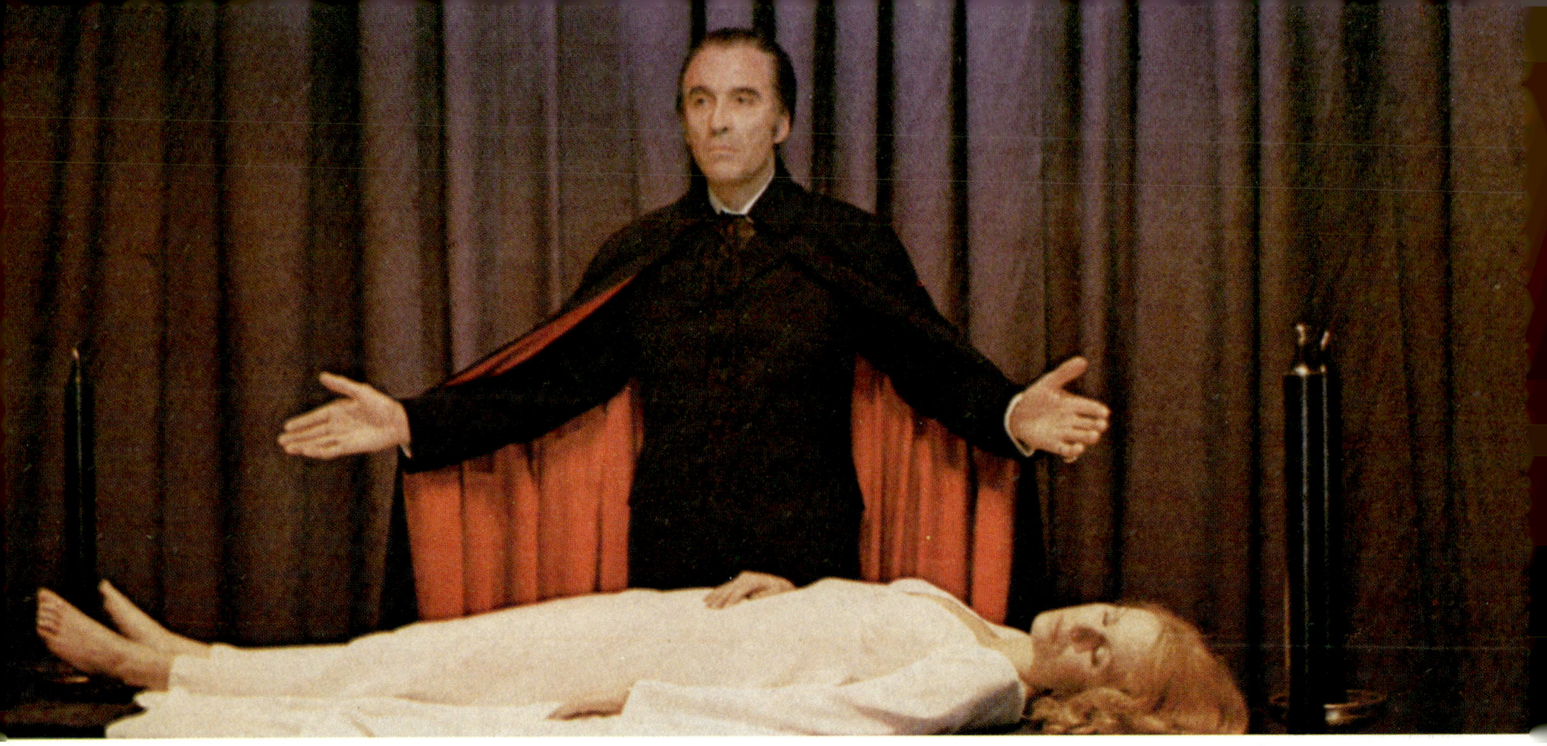

ABOVE LEFT *Ready for the kill. Lee and intended victim in* The Satanic Rites of Dracula *(Hammer 1973).*
LEFT *In search of the vampire. Checking the coffin from* Blacula *(AIP 1972).*
ABOVE *The vampire that walked the West. Undead gunslinger Michael Pate in* Curse of the Undead *(Universal 1959).*

a prosaic murder mystery. Even with Lugosi and the addition of his daughter, the Vampire Girl (Carol Borland), plus MGM production values and superb photography from James Wong Howe, *Mark of the Vampire* must ultimately be judged a failure because of the 'cheat ending' which dissipated the horror effects of Lugosi's performance and the bizarre bat-winged flight of the Vampire Girl, swung out over the set like a malevolent Peter Pan!

With *The Devil Bat* (US 1940) Lugosi began to fall victim of his own screen horror image. He played a mad scientist raising vampire bats trained to suck their victims' blood on cue. He was no doubt relieved to fall victim to one of his own creations. The genre of the vampire was already beginning to deteriorate, readying itself for impalation by Abbott and Costello!

By 1943, Lugosi was with Columbia for *The Return of The Vampire.* Tracked down as a vampire, Lugosi is correctly impaled in his grave. His return as Armand Tesla, a notorious Rumanian vampire, is brought about when a German bomb exposes the staked Tesla, and blitz workmen innocently remove the stake, reviving Tesla after 20 years beneath London. Lugosi carries on much as before, as well as turning Matt Willis into a werewolf, an action he must have regretted as Willis finally turns on him and drags him out to melt away in the sunlight. The last major appearance of Lugosi as Count Dracula was in 1948, in the inevitable *Abbott and Costello Meet Frankenstein,* shown in Britain as *Meet the Ghosts.* It is sad to reflect that Lugosi's 'death' at the hands of Abbott and Costello was brought about by Universal Pictures, who had started him on his screen stardom as Count Dracula. The definitive Count Dracula for the Thirties and Forties had reached the end of his career. The genre was to lie dormant until the colour revival by Hammer with Christopher Lee as the new Count Dracula. Before 1958, there were a few inconsequential vampire films, the most depressing being *Mother Riley meets The Vampire* with Lugosi mechanically going through the motions. In 1956, Lugosi died in a State institution from the effects of drugs and poverty.

One extraordinary vampire film made outside the United States deserves notice. This was Carl Dreyer's *Vampyr* made in 1931, the same year as Lugosi's *Dracula. Vampyr* is extraordinary for many reasons. It was privately financed by a young French film enthusiast, Baron Nicholas de Gunzburg, who was to play a leading role in the film under the pseudonym of 'Julian West'. The script was adapted from the Irish writer Sheridan Le Fanu's *Carmilla,* and the director, Dreyer, was Danish! Yet from an apparently rootless base, without the facilities of major or professional actors, Dreyer fashioned a unique film, full of implied rather than explicit horror. The strange, almost dreamlike quality of the film is as much the result of its convoluted and never very clear plot as its treatment. The use of non-professional actors, always a danger, works against the effect of the film, in some cases weakening potentially horrific scenes. The hero, played by the film's backer, is particularly undisciplined and ineffective in many scenes, so that the film relies almost entirely upon its hallucinatory images, contrasted with the solid reality of its settings. The film was made entirely on location: the inn in which the hero spends his first haunted night was a real inn; a chateau was hired for the film, as was a deserted ice factory, the house of 'dancing shadows', and the mill in which the villainous doctor finally met his death was a plaster works. Dreyer's story of vampirism was made all the more terrifying for being played against these patently solid locations.

The hero, David Gray, spends a night at a lonely inn where a room has been mysteriously booked for him. During the night he is awakened by a strange

ABOVE *Christopher Lee begins to feed in* Taste the Blood of Dracula *(Hammer 1970).*
BELOW *Corruption comes at the end in* The Satanic Rites of Dracula *(Hammer 1973).*
RIGHT *Mueller (Laurence Payne) is attacked by Emil (Anthony Corlan) as he attempts to pull the stake from the corpse of Count Mitterhouse (Robert Tayman) in* Vampire Circus *(Hammer 1971).*

old man who enters his room and gives him a parcel, telling Gray to open the parcel in the event of the stranger's death. Unable to sleep after this episode, Gray leaves the inn to wander into a strange white building filled with the dancing shadows of a witches' sabbath. The music ends abruptly, and the shadows disappear when an old woman enters the building with the village doctor.

The next day, Gray visits the chateau to find that its owner is the man who had left him the mysterious parcel at the inn. Living with him are his two daughters, Gisele and Leonie, the latter suffering from a strange debilitating illness. A shot is fired and the old man dies in the arms of Gisele. Opening the parcel, Gray finds a book on vampires and how to destroy them, entitled *Strange Tales of Vampires*.

Later in the night, Leonie is found unconscious in the castle grounds, the woman by her side. The doctor asks Gray to give blood for a transfusion to help save the girl's life. This he does, and as a result suffers a horrific nightmare in which he is placed in a coffin, onto which the lid is screwed with chilling squeaks. Through a small glass window in the lid the camera, as Gray, sees the old woman peer down in triumph, and the swaying trees above the coffin as it is carried to the cemetery. This 'first person' camera sequence is disturbingly chilling and in sheer horror makes up for the many unexplained holes in the film's plot and the inadequate acting of many of the main actors.

Gray regains consciousness in the cemetery, where his delirium has led him, and realizes that the old woman is the vampire and the doctor her accomplice. Using the book on vampires as his guide Gray finds the coffin of the old woman in the cemetery and, with the aid of one of the castle servants, he drives the traditional stake through her heart. Her apparently fresh and living body crumbles to dust, and Leonie is released from her affliction. In another scene of horror, the doctor dies, trapped in a cage in a flour mill, in a cascade of white dust that envelopes, chokes and buries him. Gray and Gisele, freed from the terrors that have surrounded them, take their lovers' walk away from the camera and into the sunlight.

The story line is vague, full of unexplained meetings, half-completed encounters and incidents that are never made clear. But the resulting film is a unique blend of mystery, gothic horror and pure horror, never quite glimpsed clearly, but carrying with it an accumulating charge of horror, released only when Gray kills the vampire woman. Even the photography, by Rudolf Mate, was deliberately ghostly, the effect being achieved by shooting all the scenes through a piece of gauze placed some three feet in front of the camera's lens. It also made all the scenes seem to take place in a monochrome limbo, neither night nor day. The end result is a vampire film which still has the power to suggest evil incarnate and hidden horrors, briefly glimpsed from the corner of the eye, or suggested by a flickering shadow or bar of music.

The vampire film had been languishing in the second feature doldrums even before Lugosi met Abbott and Costello and once more it was Hammer Films who put new blood into the genre when in 1958 they made *Dracula* (US title: *The Horror of Dracula*) in colour. With two great stars for the price of one, Lee playing Dracula with charm and evil panache, and Cushing, like a coiled spring and single-minded as Van Helsing, the eternal nemesis of the vampire, *Dracula* became an even greater box-office success than Hammer's *The Curse of Frankenstein*. Cushing and Lee were established for all time as world stars, Lee taking over the role created by Lugosi and making it his own, while Cushing made the role of Van Helsing totally credible, a worthy adversary for the Count.

Once again, Jimmy Sangster wrote the screenplay, and Fisher directed. One national critic dubbed it 'The most distinguished horror film ever made'. Again, Fisher deliberately avoided both the original book and the original film in his approach. As a result Lee's Dracula is a creature with sweeping, athletic movements far more effective than any change into a flapping bat. As Fisher says, 'Dracula is tremendously sensual. This is one of the great attractions of evil. The first time you see Dracula, he is at the top of the staircase and in silhouette. The audience, the ones you want to laugh, start to laugh because they think they're going to see fangs, the eyes, and everything else. Dracula comes downstairs, into close-up and they see this handsome, charming and totally attractive man. This was done with a purpose, not just to kid them but to show that the whole idea of evil is very attractive. It's one of the great cards that evil holds!'

Lee became the definitive Count Dracula for a generation of horror addicts to whom Lugosi was merely a name from television films or society shows. To his handsome gaunt height, accentuated by the swirling cloak and, in the climactic scenes, the dripping fangs and blood-red eyes, Lee added his own concept of Dracula. He made the character 'acceptable', by stressing along with the very deep evil of the man, his nobility, austerity, and, above all, his totally irresistible appeal to women. The sexual attraction of the vampire legend, hinted at

Lee attacks Valerie Gaunt in Terry Fisher's superb colour production of Dracula *(Hammer 1958).*

in the first cycle of vampire films, was now quite overt.

The film's final scene, a vicious, physical duel between Dracula and Van Helsing, with the latter attempting the destruction of the vampire becomes a duel of titans and a worthy climax to this classic film. Van Helsing has followed the Count to Castle Dracula, and traps Dracula as he bursts into the study, trying to seek the sanctuary of the castle's catacombs before dawn comes. In a scene that has yet to be surpassed in subsequent Dracula films (and, in fact, Hammer used the scene again as a prologue to their *Dracula, Prince of Darkness* in 1965), Lee and Cushing made physical the manifestations of the battle of good against evil. Van Helsing finally forces Dracula, inch by inch, into a shaft of sunlight in which the Count disintegrates horribly into a heap of dust, some lank hair drifting in the wind, and a signet ring glinting in the cleansing light.

Cushing made some suggestions, in keeping with the characterization and style of the film. He says: 'In the first Dracula picture I suggested that it is always good to have some sort of almost Douglas Fairbanks scene . . . have a jolly good leap and a lunge . . . towards the end, just before Chris Lee disintegrated, the script just said that Van Helsing gets out his crucifix and forces Dracula into the sunlight. I said it would be absolutely marvellous if they could jump off a balcony onto the curtains. They couldn't construct a balcony because of the expense and the fact that the set had already been built, so what we did was to have a long refectory table. I ran along it and leaped as far as I could and pulled the curtains down, which was more visually effective than just running to them and pulling them down.'

In Britain, on release, the film achieved the curious distinction of causing the greatest number of its audiences to faint.

Fisher directed the next Hammer Dracula picture, *The Brides of Dracula* (1960). Cushing gave another fine performance as the vampire hunter Van Helsing, with David Peel playing Baron Meinster, the chief vampire, whose mother (Martita Hunt) keeps him chained in the castle, and lures young girls there to satisfy his vampire lusts. A young girl, Marianne, becomes a guest at the castle when she is stranded at the local inn. Feeling sorry for the young Baron described by his mother as 'sick and feeble-minded' Marianne frees him. The handsome young baron follows Marianne back to her school and while 'courting' her, spreads vampirism liberally among her all-too-willing schoolfriends. The Baroness becomes a vampire as the result of an incestuous attack by her son, and one of the finest moments of horror in the film is where, nervous as a schoolgirl with her first date, the Baroness removes her veil to show Van Helsing her hideous vampire fangs. Yet another terrible moment occurs as the Baron's crazed nurse with promises of unmentionable pleasures coaxes the 'corpse' of one of the Baron's female victims to leave the protection of the grave and follow Meinster.

Van Helsing himself, for a terrifying instant, becomes infected with the taint of the vampire after Meinster attacks him. Cushing superbly conveys the agony of a man suffering not only the physical but the spiritual pains of the damned as he burns the vampire's bite from his flesh with a white hot poker. This is a scene which still has the power to hold an audience silent and horror stricken. At the climax of the film, Baron Meinster is killed when Van Helsing manipulates the sails of a windmill to form a shadow of the Cross on the vampire.

The success of *Dracula* in 1958 brought a spate of Vampire films, such as *Tempi Duri per i Vampiri* (Italy 1962), shown as *Uncle was a Vampire* in America, starring Christopher Lee, by now the international Count Dracula. In 1964 there was an Italian-American co-production of Richard Matherson's terrifying novel *I am Legend*, filmed with Vincent Price as *The Last Man on Earth*. Price played the sole survivor of a plague which has turned the rest of its victims into vampire-like zombies. He lives alone in his barricaded house, further protected by mirrors and garlic at the door. He is shocked to meet a girl immune to the garlic and it is only when he finds her about to inject herself that she reveals herself to be one of a group of survivors who have found an antidote to the plague. This group, whose members have been killed by Price along with his destruction of the infected vampire/zombies, finally murders Price who has by then 'cursed' the girl with a transfusion of his own untainted blood. The last man on earth is dead. The film's basic premise held a great deal of impact and overt horror, not all of which was realized in a production marred by poor technical work and inept dialogue. It held sufficient charge of horror, however, to warrant a remake in 1971 with Charlton Heston as *The Omega Man*, fighting for his existence in a Los Angeles turned into a ghost town by the effect of germ warfare between Russia and China.

In 1962, with *Kiss of the Vampire* (US title: *Kiss of Evil*), Hammer returned with a minor masterpiece of the genre, this time directed by Australian Don Sharp and with the chief vampire, Dr. Ravna being played with courteous menace by Noel Willman. It began traditionally enough with a stranded honeymoon couple foolishly accepting the hospitality of Dr. Ravna in his luxurious chateau, only later discovering that the chateau is the headquarters of the vampires in the area. Professor Zimmer (Clifford Evans) finally traps the vampires in the ritual chamber in the castle, having smeared all the exits with garlic. There is a magnificent and horrifying final sequence when thousands of huge bats, summoned by Zimmer's incantations, swoop down on the castle, destroying Ravna and his trapped disciples.

Amicus Films, now a British-based film company sent up the vampire legend in one of their compendium films *Dr. Terror's House of Horrors* (GB 1965). In the episode *Vampire*, written by one of the film's producers, Milton Subotsky, Donald Sutherland, as the new doctor in a small American town, finds himself married to a vampire and seeks help from fellow-practitioner, Dr. Blake, whose unexceptional advice is for Sutherland to destroy his vampire wife in the usual manner. Having driven a stake through her heart, Sutherland then finds himself charged with his wife's murder, his story of vampirism unconfirmed by Dr. Blake, who, as Sutherland is taken away, muses to himself: 'There isn't room for two doctors and two vampires in a small town', before he takes to the air as a bat!

LEFT *Charlton Heston menaced by the Undead in* The Omega Man *(Seltzer 1971).*
In Don Sharp's Kiss of Evil *(Hammer 1962), the unwary travellers, Jennifer Daniel and Edward De Souza, are greeted by Noel Willman as Dr. Ravna* (above) *and are given protection from the vampire by a priest, Noel Howlett* (below).

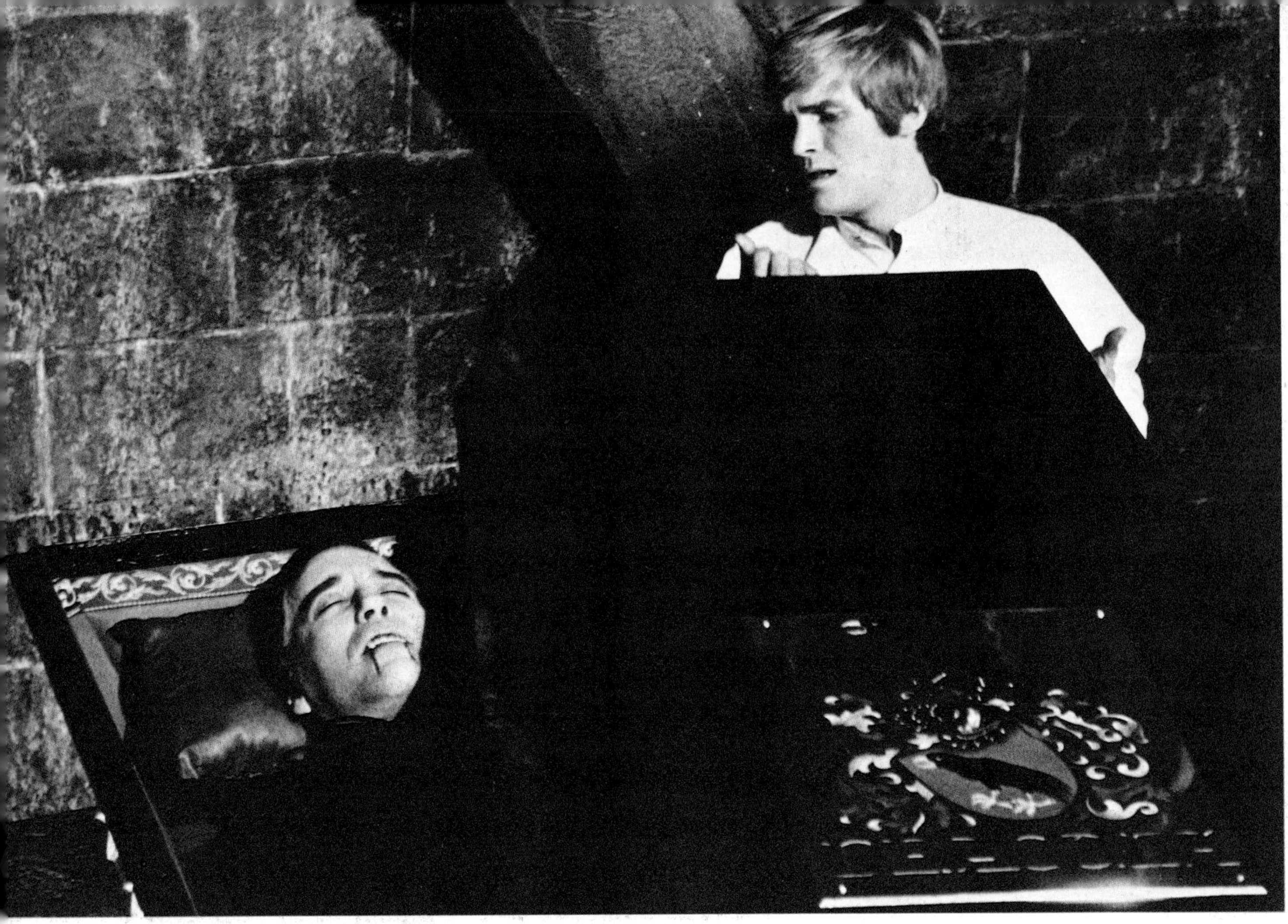

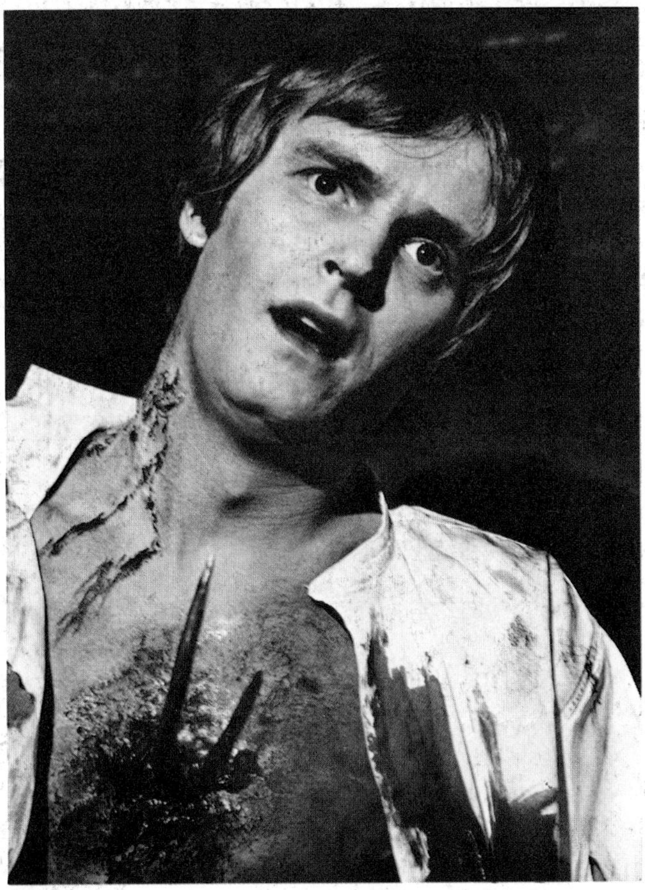

Christopher Matthews (above) *discovers the resting vampire, Christopher Lee, and is later horribly murdered* (left) *by the Count in* Scars of Dracula *(Hammer/EMI 1970)*.
OPPOSITE TOP LEFT *Dracula awakens from his coffin in Freddie Francis'* Dracula Has Risen From the Grave *(Hammer 1968)*.
TOP RIGHT *Lee attacks in* Dracula, Prince of Darkness *(Hammer-Seven Arts 1965)*.
RIGHT *Ferdy Mayne as the vampire Count von Krolok in Roman Polanski's* Dance of the Vampires *(Cadre/Filmways 1967)*.
FAR RIGHT *Jon Pertwee* (left) *tries on the genuine vampire's cloak in* The House That Dripped Blood *(Amicus 1970)*.

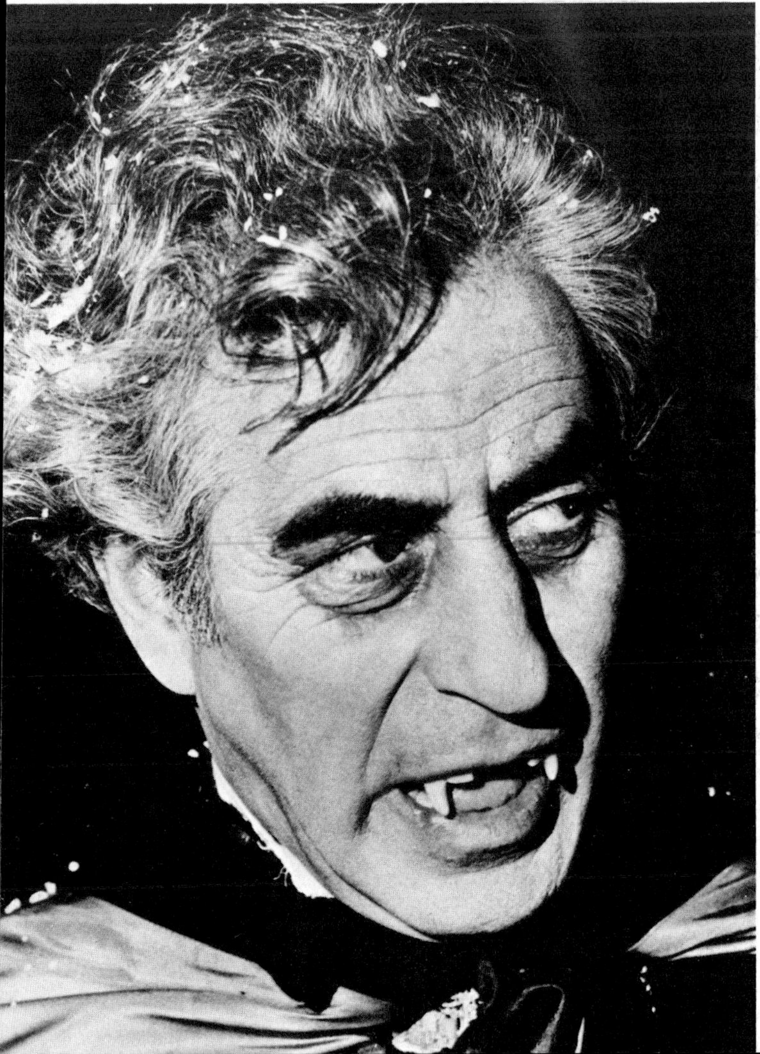

With *Dance of the Vampires* Polish director Roman Polanski attempted, not too successfully, to make a feature-length spoof of the vampire film. Some of the jokes work, such as the screen credit which reads 'Fangs by Dr. Ludwig von Krankheit', and the scene where the obligatory hunchback Koukol (played by ex-boxing champion Terry Downes) is menaced by a wolf in an empty snow-scape. After a snarling encounter with the wolf, he returns from behind a snowdrift with the remains of the wolf still dripping from his happy mouth. In a complex and over-clever plot, the film fails to jell as either parody or horror, although Ferdy Mayne makes an excellent vampire Count. The set pieces have an inherent horror which goes against the generally jokey grain of the film—as in the dance of the vampires itself, with the guests emerging formally from their coffins to dance stately minuets at the ball, until brought to an abrupt halt when all but the interloping humans are rendered invisible in front of a panoramic mirror.

In 1966 Lee returned in Hammer's *Dracula—Prince of Darkness* which Terence Fisher directed with his customary skill and effective use of colour and horror. The film lacked Cushing's Van Helsing to provide Dracula with a worthy opponent, except in the prologue, a re-run of the ending of *Dracula*. We then become witness to Dracula's rather gory revival. His faithful manservant Klove (Philip Latham) suspends yet another unwary guest of Castle Dracula over the catafalque containing the Count's ashes. Klove then slits open the unfortunate guest's stomach, the resulting deluge of blood on the ashes reconstituting Count Dracula. Dracula is soon up to his usual activities, rapidly making up for his ten-year absence from the Carpathian mountains. Eventually in an escape attempt he topples from the wagon Klove is driving into the castle's ice-covered moat. The ice is broken by a fusillade of shots from his pursuers and Count Dracula perishes again, for the first time by water.

You can't keep a good vampire down for long, and Lee was back again as Dracula in 1970 in *Scars of Dracula*, directed this time by Roy Ward Baker. It contains moments of pure terror, particularly as Dracula climbs the wall of his castle, pinned to it like a monstrous lizard. This time he receives his destruction from the heavens themselves when, as he is about to impale a victim on a spike, it is struck by lightning and, wrapped in flames, Dracula falls from the castle battlements to the ravine below.

In 1970 Hammer turned their attention to the female of the species with *The Vampire Lovers*. Full frontal vampirism, previously hinted at, at last

reached the screen in this film, yet another adaptation of Sheridan Le Fanu's *Carmilla*. What had been implicit in Dreyer's *Vampyr* now erupted in an orgy of lesbianism, naked breasts and horror. Cushing appears as General Spielsdorf into whose home the vampiress Mircalla, now known as Marcilla, comes to kill his daughter, after which, changing her name to Carmilla, she proceeds to yet another home where she becomes the 'bosom' friend of the General's late daughter. As the girl begins to languish from Carmilla's fanged attentions, the vampiress attempts to retain her hold by making vampires of her doctor, governess and the butler! Little surprise then, when she is finally despatched first by the vampire killer Baron Hartog (Douglas Wilmer), who plunges a stake through her heart and then by Cushing who beheads her for good measure!

The year 1971 started promisingly with another episode from a multi-story film from Amicus, wittily and deftly directed by Peter Duffell, *The House that Dripped Blood*. In *The Cloak*, Jon Pertwee, playing Paul Henderson, the great vampire actor, decides that the production values of his latest horror epic are not up to his standard. He

The ladies get fangs. Yutte Stensgaard (above) *has a bite in* Lust for a Vampire *(Hammer 1970), while Ingrid Pitt* (below) *takes a rest in Roy Ward Baker's* The Vampire Lovers *(Hammer/AIP 1970).*

buys a new vampire's cloak from a delighted costumier and is horrified to discover that he turns into a genuine vampire when he puts it on. He levitates at midnight, turns his co-star Ingrid Pitt into a vampire, and finds it impossible to stop his neck-biting activities on the film set when the director shouts 'Cut'. Ruefully, Henderson remarks: 'I've been playing vampires for years, but I've never actually *bitten* anyone before.' Finally, after a hilarious fight in the basement of a house with the police inspector, he dies as the inspector impales him, only to be vampirized himself by Ingrid Pitt. With everything understated, even the parody of the horror film 'within-a-film' itself, the episode works effectively both as a vampire film with moments of genuine horror, and as a witty send-up of the whole genre.

America realized the potentialities of the renewed vampire cycle, and 1970 brought their own titled vampire in *Count Yorga, Vampire.* Set in contemporary Los Angeles, its horror became all the more effective for being treated in an unsensational way. Robert Quarry made a convincing vampire, and in a welter of deaths, the hero ends up in an appropriately downbeat manner, discovering the girlfriend he has rescued has herself become a vampire. Quarry was back again in *The Return of Count Yorga* (US 1971) and in fine fettle. After meeting with a young boy from an orphanage in a graveyard, naturally, the Count attends a fancy dress party at the orphanage, vaguely surprised that half the male guests come dressed as vampires. Despite the carnage he creates around him, with his hordes of vampires setting off at regular intervals to massacre various enemies of Yorga, the Count himself is seen fully aware of his contemporary situation, watching a television showing of *The Vampire Lovers*! The violent end is routine, with police and vampire hunter battling with the vampire hordes, and Yorga being thrown by the vampire hunter to his death from a balcony. Only the ending remains the same: as the heroine turns in gratitude to the

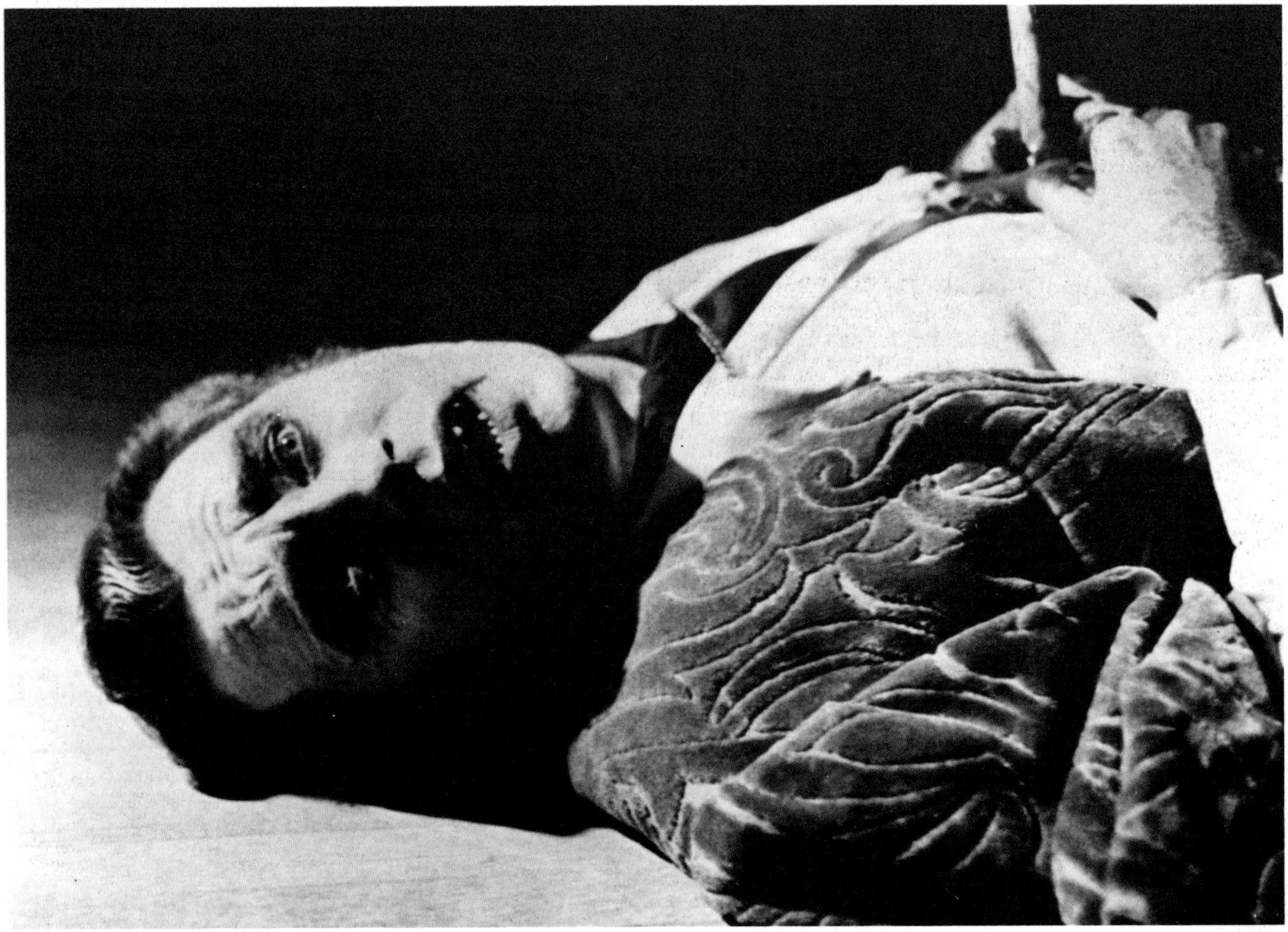

ABOVE *American vampire Robert Quarry dies in the title role of* Count Yorga, Vampire *(Erica/AIP 1970).*
RIGHT *Christopher Lee prepares to sink his fangs into a tempting jugular vein in* Taste the Blood of Dracula *(Hammer 1970).*

ABOVE *Klaus Klinski stakes his claim as a fearless vampire killer in* Count Dracula *(Fenix/Corona/Filmar/Towers 1970).*
BELOW *Count Dracula dies for the first time, impaled on a broken wheel spoke, in* Dracula A.D. 1972 *(Hammer 1972).*
RIGHT *Marty Feldman, Vampire!* Every Home Should Have One *(Example 1970).*

vampire killer, Dr. Baldwin, she finds that he, too, has become a vampire!

With *Dracula A.D. 1972* (GB 1972), there was an uneasy and none-too-effective attempt by Hammer to transfer Count Dracula to contemporary Chelsea. The most horrifying sequence occurred at the beginning, set in 1872, with a struggle to the death on a coach drawn by runaway horses, between Count Dracula and Van Helsing. Both were killed in this struggle, Dracula transfixed by a broken spoke from one of the coach's shattered wheels. In the contemporary story which follows, Dracula (Christopher Lee) is revived by Johnny Alucard (Christopher Neame) in a desanctified church, only to be fought and destroyed by Cushing as a descendant of Van Helsing, this time uneasily in league with the forces of Scotland Yard. Van Helsing's granddaughter becomes the main target for Dracula, and in following her, Cushing disposes of young Alucard by means of water (he falls backwards into a bath!) and, after a violent fight with Lee in the ruined church, manages to despatch the Count by throwing a phial of holy water at him, leaving Lee to decay and disintegrate in time-honoured fashion.

Back again in a contemporary setting, Van Helsing is called in by the British Security Forces in *The Satanic Rites of Dracula* (GB 1973) to investigate black magic ceremonies involving, topically, a senior government minister. Cushing soon finds out, in a country house filled with female vampires lying in wait in their coffins, that he is faced once again with Count Dracula. After many bouts of bloodthirsty activity Cushing despatches Lee into his regular pile of dust. Here again the setting of Lee and Cushing in a contemporary situation militated against a really vintage Dracula, but there is little doubt that Lee and Cushing will continue to cover the various new and more gory permutations of the vampire film.

ABOVE *Van Helsing versus Dracula. Peter Cushing protects Stephanie Beacham from Christopher Lee in* Dracula A.D. 1972 *(Hammer 1972).*
TOP RIGHT *Vonette McGee cowers from the Undead in* Blacula *(AIP 1972).*
RIGHT *Rank Film Distributors' poster for* The Twins of Evil *(Hammer 1971).*

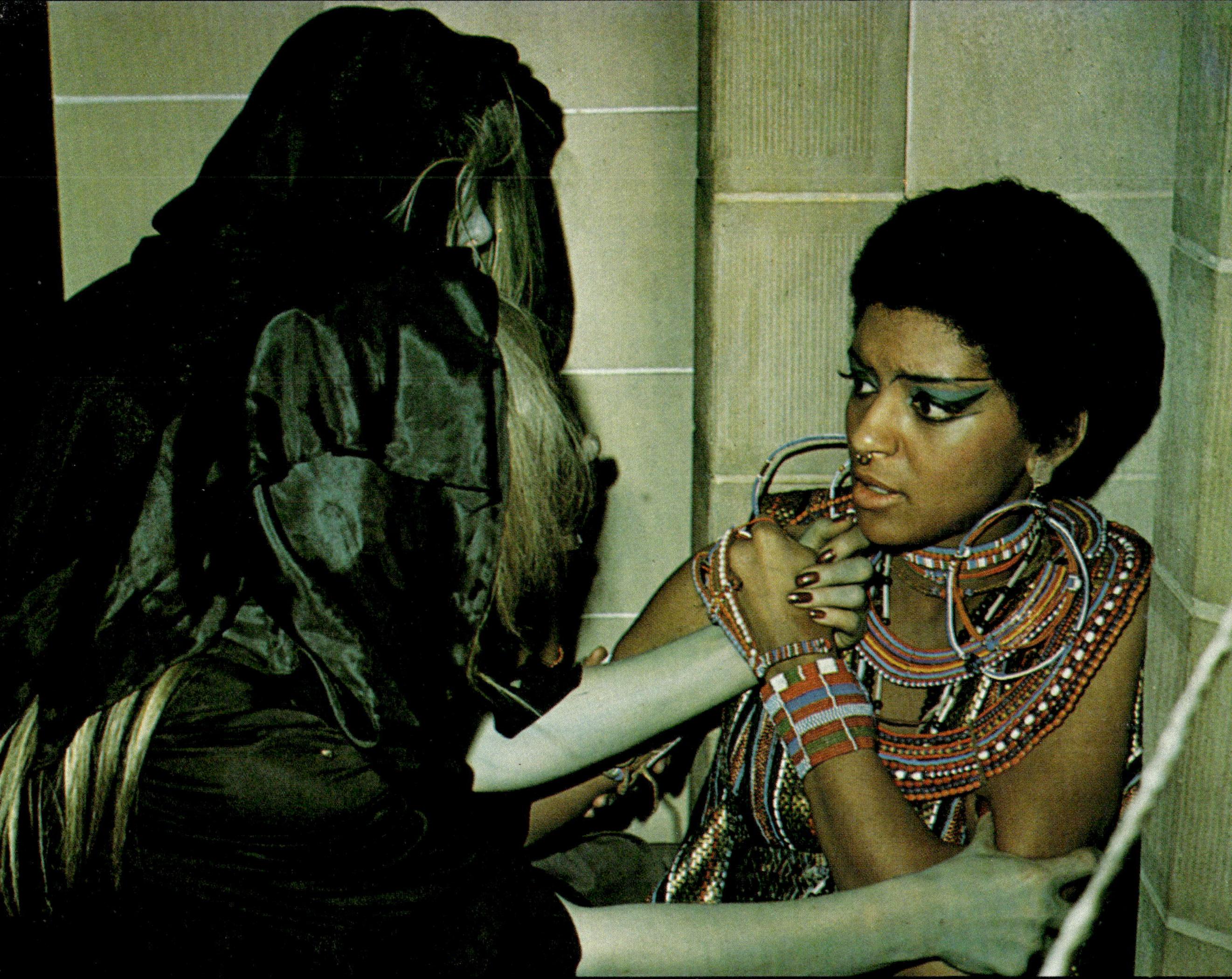

HAMMER HORROR
A NEW TERROR-FILLED X FILM
TWINS OF EVIL
RANK FILM DISTRIBUTORS PRESENTS
A HAMMER PRODUCTION
"TWINS OF EVIL" X
STARRING
PETER CUSHING
CO-STARRING
DENNIS PRICE
ALSO STARRING
MADELEINE & MARY COLLINSON
ISOBEL BLACK · KATHLEEN BYRON
DAMIEN THOMAS · DAVID WARBECK
SCREENPLAY BY TUDOR GATES PRODUCED BY HARRY FINE AND MICHAEL STYLE
DIRECTED BY JOHN HOUGH COLOUR

RANK FILM DISTRIBUTORS PRESENT
A HAMMER FILM PRODUCTION
VAMPIRE CIRCUS
X
ADRIENNE CORRI · LAURENCE PAYNE
ANTHONY CORLAN
THORLEY WALTERS · JOHN MOULDER-BROWN
ALSO STARRING
LYNNE FREDERICK · RICHARD OWENS · ELIZABETH SEAL
SCREENPLAY BY JUDSON KINBERG
PRODUCED BY WILBUR STARK
DIRECTED BY ROBERT YOUNG
COLOUR

½ DOZEN
4233/____0
LAMP FOUNT ASST.

By now, Lee had become firmly established as Count Dracula, tall, gaunt, exuding sheer evil and sexual magnetism in equal amounts. As a result, *Count Dracula*, the film version of Bram Stoker's original *Dracula*, which stuck closely to Stoker's conception of the character, proved unsuccessful when finally released in Britain in 1973. Although it was a role Lee had wanted to play for many years, by now audiences were unwilling to accept him in any image other than the one he had created from *Dracula* onwards, and certainly not as the middle-aged and bewhiskered Count Dracula. The film's low budget militated against its success.

The new wave of 'black' films gave birth to the first negro vampire, in *Blacula* (US 1972). When in 1815 African Prince Mamuwalde (William Marshall) asks Count Dracula to sign a petition abolishing slavery, Dracula's reply was brief and to the point. 'I curse you with my name—you will be BLACULA, ,a vampire like myself. A living fiend!' Sealed in a coffin for a century and a half, torn by an unquenchable desire for blood, he is released in contemporary America by two young homosexual decorators out to make a quick buck from the antiques they purchased from Castle Dracula. They become the first victims of the evil Blacula, and probably the first gay vampires in screen history! Soon the city is awash with vampires—they are finally killed when their resting place is set on fire by the vampire hunter and police lieutenant. Inadvertently, they kill Blacula's love with a stake, whereupon Blacula, his love gone, decides to end it all, walking into the deadly rays of the rising sun, there to decompose.

However bizarre or outrageous the film, the one certainty is that Dracula and all his vampire cohorts will continue to terrify screen audiences for as long as horror films are made, and the Count will continue to justify his position as one of the most international, and horrifying monsters of terror.

PRECEDING PAGES *Horror strikes in the domain of the vampire. Two scenes from* Taste the Blood of Dracula *(Hammer 1970).*
LEFT *Rank Film Distributors' poster for* Vampire Circus *(Hammer 1972).*
BELOW LEFT *William Marshall in the title role runs amok in* Blacula *(AIP 1972).*
BELOW *The destruction of Count Dracula. Christopher Lee faces death in* The Satanic Rites of Dracula *(Hammer 1973).*

ABOVE *Daniel Massey ends up as 'blood from the tap' in* Vault of Horror *(Metromedia/Amicus 1973).*
BELOW *Count Dracula comes to Tokyo! Two scenes from* Lake of Dracula *(Toho 1971).*
RIGHT *Christopher Lee untypically as the bewhiskered Count envisaged by Bram Stoker in* Count Dracula *(Fenix/Corona/Filmar/Towers 1970).*

BACK FROM THE DEAD

"This is the Scroll of Thoth. Herein are set down the magic words by which Isis raised Osiris from the dead . . . We live today . . . We shall live again. In many forms we shall return . . . !" The Mummy (*US 1932*)

THE MUMMY makes an ideal film monster. Raised from death after thousands of years in the tomb, decay and corruption held back by the bandages and caked dust, the mummy has the unstoppable power of an automaton. Only the eyes, burning with the memory of love and with evil give the mummy its likeness to man and thus its power to chill. So it was natural that after the successes of *Dracula* and *Frankenstein*, Universal should cast Karloff, their new horror star, in *The Mummy* (US 1932).

From the earliest days, the cinema had been fascinated with the subject of ancient Egypt. Georges Méliès, the great French maker of 'fantastic' and 'trick' films had conjured up *Cleopatra* (France 1899) in which an evil old man, after hacking a mummy to bits, had used fire to resuscitate the living woman! In 1901 the British film-maker, Walter R. Booth—like Méliès, formerly a magician—made the *Haunted Curiosity Shop* in which, before the very eyes of a scholar and the horrified audience, a living mummy appeared. First its wrappings fell away to disclose the living Egyptian: in turn his flesh melted slowly until only the skeleton remained! In Germany in 1918 Emil Jannings, later to be one of the screen's greatest stars and winner of one of the first Academy Awards, played the title role in *Die Augen der Mumie Ra* ('The Eyes of The Mummy'), scaring the senses from Pola Negri! But it was Karloff and make-up man Jack Pierce who were to revive the mummy cycle in 1932, adding another 'classic' horror role to those played by Karloff. Like Lee in 1959, Karloff was only to play the part once, making it uniquely his own.

In *The Mummy* Karloff was Im-ho-tep, revived after 3,700 years when British archaeologist Bramwell Fletcher unwittingly reads the potent words of the sacred Book of Thoth. As he reads, the parchment eyelids of the mummy slowly open, and a hand reaches out, its fingertips crumbling with the decay of centuries in the tomb. Leaving a trail of rotting bandages, the mummy moves inexorably out of the tomb with the sacred scroll, while Fletcher, his insane laughter filling the vault, cries out: 'He went for a little walk!' This little walk was the first of one of the more resilient monsters of horror.

Im-ho-tep, with incredibly shrivelled features, next appears ten years later, wearing a fez, as the Egyptian archaeologist Ardet Bey who helps David Manners to discover the tomb of Princess Anck-es-en-Amon. It was for his sacrilege in attempting to raise the Princess whom he loved that Im-ho-tep had been buried alive with the Scroll of Thoth. To Zita Johann, the daughter of the Governor of Sudan, who is the reincarnation of Im-ho-tep's lost love, Ardet Bey shows the scenes of Im-ho-tep's terrible love and even more terrible punishment on the surface of a pool. He intends the death of the girl in order to reunite Im-ho-tep with Anck-es-en-Amon, but as he tries to transfer her soul to the mummy of his beloved princess, Zita calls on the Goddess Isis for help. A statue crashes and Karloff becomes dust.

Directed by Karl Freund, the film conveyed all the horror of the creature beyond the grave, with Karloff superb both as the mummy and as the eerie and shrivelled Ardet Bey. The full-length mummy is seldom seen, horror being conveyed with close-up shots of head, shoulders and hands, covered with rotting bandages and ancient flaking clay. The combination of Karloff—billed by surname only as 'Karloff the Uncanny' (an honour previously only accorded to Garbo!)—Freund, Pierce and magnificent photography credited to Charles Stumar, *The Mummy* was to remain the key film of the genre.

Karloff was to play the mummy only once, leaving to others the sequels which came in the Forties as Universal scoured previous successes for low-cost second-feature material. First was *The Mummy's Hand* (1940) in which Im-ho-tep has become Kharis, a Prince who loves the Princess Ananka. On her death he steals the sacred tana leaves whose juice has the power to revive the dead. Caught and buried alive, he has his tongue cut out '. . . so the ears of the Gods would not be assailed by his un-

LEFT *Christopher Lee as Kharis, the High Priest, before his tongue is cut out and he is mummified in* The Mummy *(Hammer 1959)*

LEFT *Boris Karloff under wraps as Im-ho-tep, the greatest of the Undead, in* The Mummy *(Universal 1932).*
ABOVE (left and right) *Before and after! Tom Baker, Michael Craig, Curt Jurgens, Terry Thomas and Daniel Massey as they are, and in Roy Ashton's horrific make-up in two scenes from* Vault of Horror *(Metromedia/Amicus 1973).*
RIGHT *Boris Karloff and Ann Revere try to contact the dead in* The Devil Commands *(Columbia 1941).*
FAR RIGHT *Bela Lugosi as Murder Legendre with Madge Bellamy in* White Zombie *(Amusement Securities 1932).*

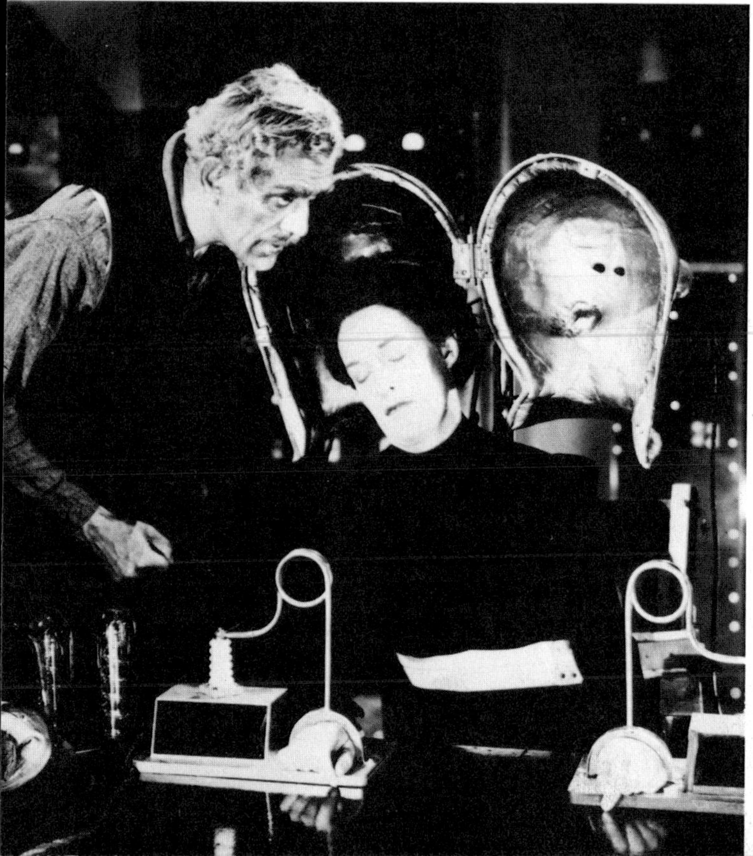

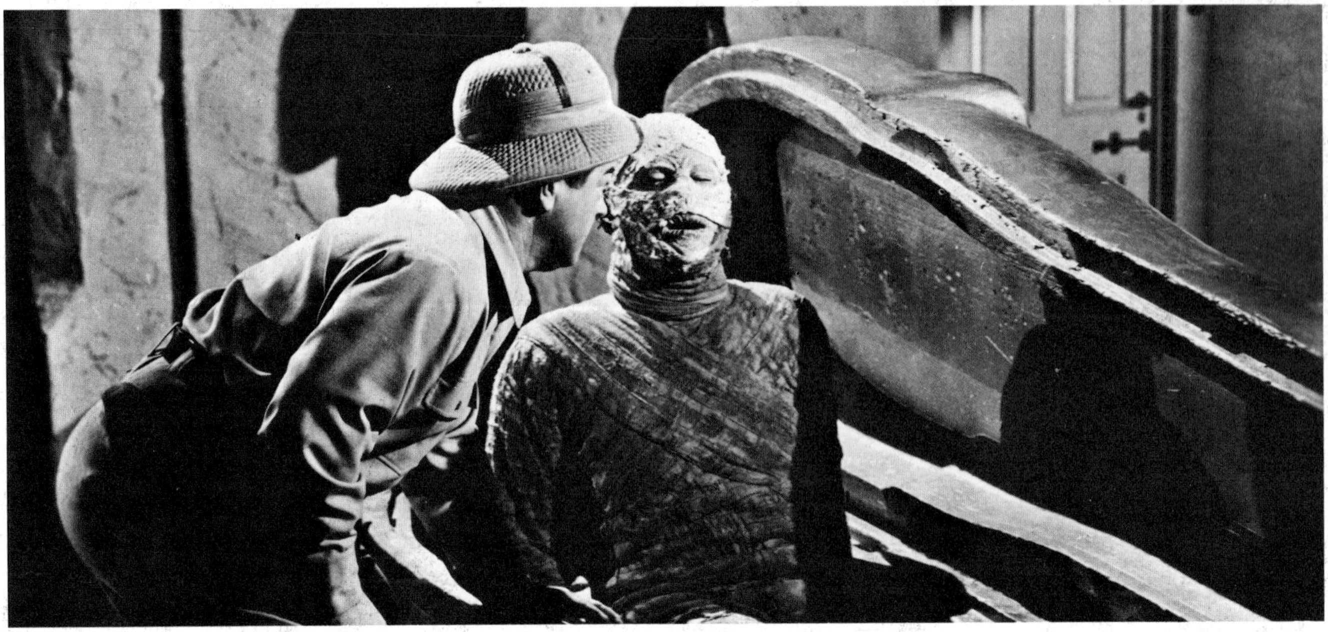

holy curses!' Kharis, kept alive by the administration of a potion of the tana leaves, guards the Princess's tomb against defilers, under the watchful eye of the new High Priest (George Zucco). Needless to say, the inevitable desecration takes place in the form of Dick Foran and Wallace Ford: Zucco feeds the mummy with a really potent brew of nine (instead of the usual three) tana leaves, to give him movement and immunity from bullets. Kharis is finally stopped only by incineration as a vat of flaming tana juice is tipped over him! Cowboy actor Tom Tyler played the mummy, chosen because of his resemblance to the young Karloff, a necessary requisite since Universal had lifted the complete incarceration sequence featuring Karloff from the original film. But Tyler, crippled with arthritis, was unable to bring to the part the power and horror that Karloff had provided.

Lon Chaney Jr next put on the bandages as High Priest Kharis, to capitalize on his new-found success as Universal's monster. In *The Mummy's Tomb* (1942) Chaney gave make-up man Pierce additional problems as Universal spliced in flashbacks with Karloff, asked for continuity with Tyler and insisted that Chaney fans should recognize their idol. Additionally, stuntman Eddie Parker took over on occasions for more strenuous activities! Little wonder that Pierce ended up by saving time and trouble with a mask! The film was but a pale shadow of the original, this time setting its action in Mapleton, Massachusetts, where the new High Priest, Turhan Bey, has brought Kharis to wreak vengeance on Dick Foran and Wallace Ford, by now white-haired. The High Priest's hopes of ensnaring beautiful Elyse Knox as his Priestess, using Kharis to capture her, come to nothing in that ever-familiar fiery climax! (Incidentally, this time the torch-bearing villagers were spliced in from *Frankenstein*!)

However much Lon Chaney hated playing The Mummy, he was Kharis again in *The Mummy's Ghost*, complete with more flashbacks as John Carradine took over the High Priesthood from George Zucco. The film was again set in Massachusetts but had nothing much new to offer, except that, reunited in the last reel with Ananka, Kharis kills the perfidious Carradine and as Ananka, like *She* before her, shrivels into old age, the two lovers sink into a swamp!

Although, as a series, the mummy was dead, Universal resuscitated it once more in *The Mummy's Curse* (1944) released only eight months after *The Mummy's Ghost*. It was the same tepid brew of tana leaves as before, only with a new High Prist (Peter Coe), a new Ananka (Virginia Christine) and a new ending—Kharis, Samson-style, brings a monastery down in ruins on everyone's head! This was to be Chaney's last venture under wraps. When, inevitably, *Abbott and Costello Meet The Mummy* was made in 1955, it was Chaney's double, Eddie Parker, who bore the brunt as Kharis! Even before this terminal encounter, the mummy had been under

ABOVE *A fate worse than death! Edwin Parker as the mummy comes face to face with Lou Costello in* Abbott and Costello Meet the Mummy *(Universal 1954).*
RIGHT *The mummy (Christopher Lee) attacks Mehemet (George Pastell) in* The Mummy *(Hammer 1959).*

ABOVE *Dickie Owen faces 3,000 year-old Terence Morgan and Jeanne Roland in Michael Carreras'* The Curse of the Mummy's Tomb *(Hammer-Swallow 1964).*
BELOW *Cowboy-star Tom Tyler, in bandages, carries on the Universal series with an armful of Peggy Moran in* The Mummy's Hand *(Universal 1940).*
RIGHT *Lon Chaney Jnr. comes back from the dead to murder in* The Mummy's Ghost *(Universal 1944).*

comic attack by Wheeler and Wolsey in *Mummy's Boys* (US 1935) and The Three Stooges in *Mummies Dummies* (US 1938), but it was Universal's insistence upon flogging a dead mummy that had really brought about the temporary demise of this screen monster.

Once more it was left to Hammer to revive the whole genre with *The Mummy* in 1959. This brought Peter Cushing and Christopher Lee back again as antagonists, under the expert direction of Terence Fisher. Jimmy Sangster's script moved the action to Victorian times, but preserved the basic story of High Priest Kharis, tongue cut out and entombed for 4,000 years to guard the tomb of the embalmed princess Ananka. Once again, the discoverer of the tomb, Stephen Banning (Felix Aylmer), is driven mad by his experience, his young son John (Peter Cushing) escaping that fate due to a leg injury which keeps him laid up in his tent as the tomb is desecrated.

Brought to England by the sinister Mehemet who brings him to life to wreak vengeance on those who desecrated the tomb of Ananka, Kharis (Christopher Lee) murders both Banning—breaking into the insane asylum to strangle him—and Whemple, another member of the expedition, before turning his attentions to John Banning. He nearly kills Banning, showing himself quite impervious to guns

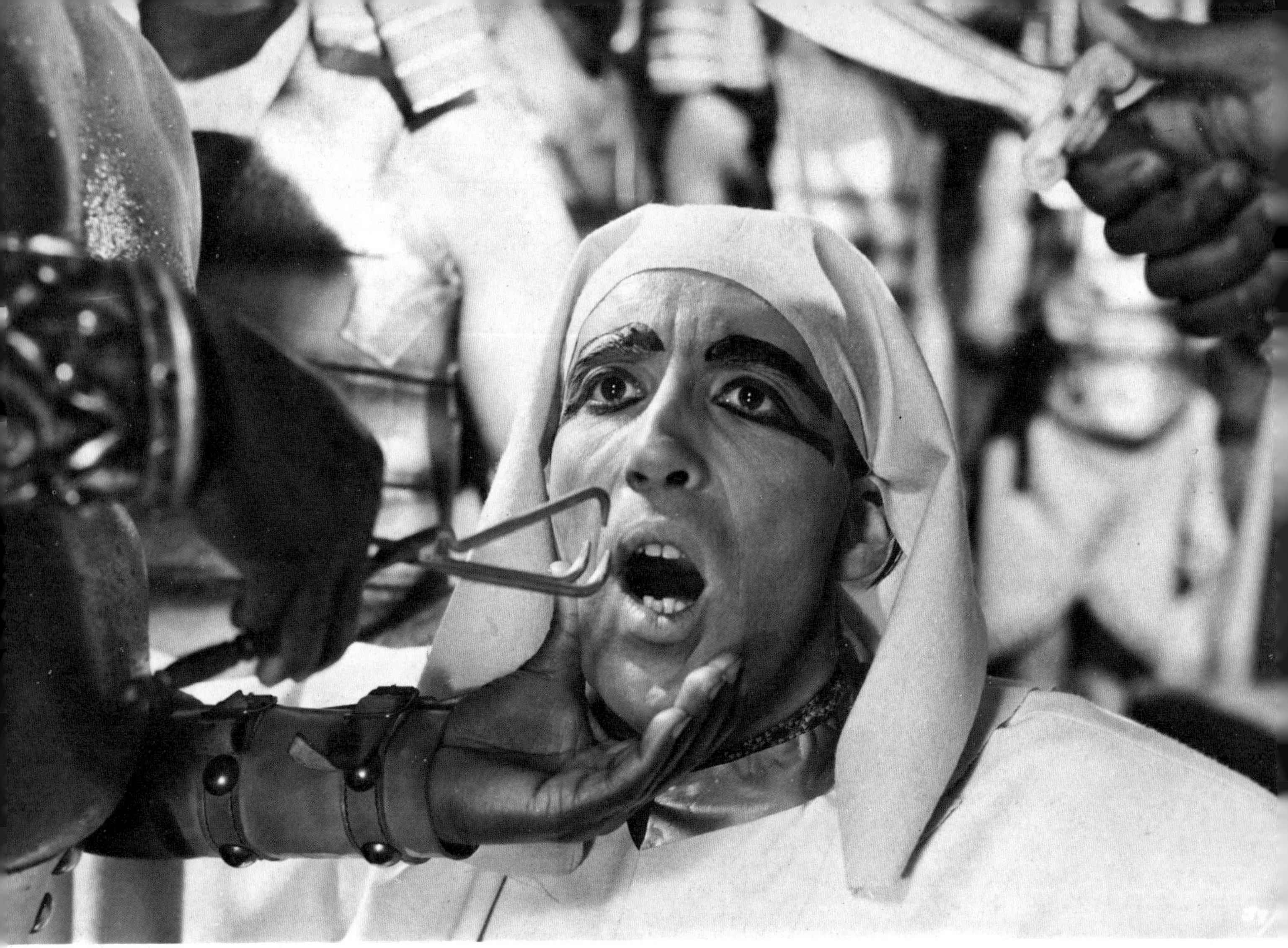

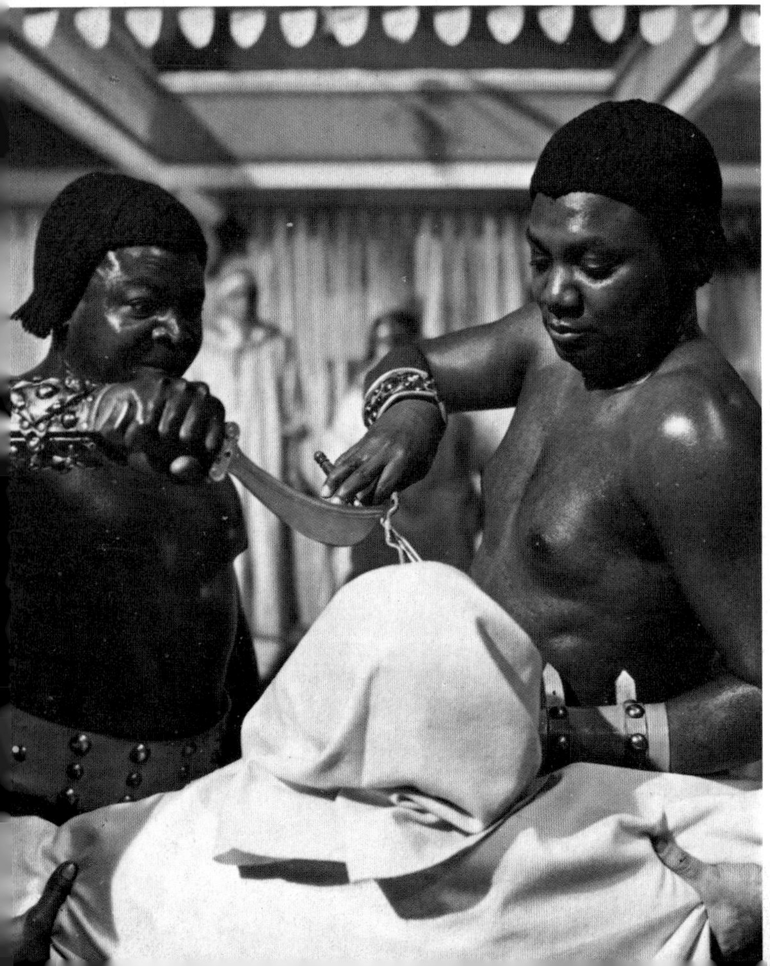

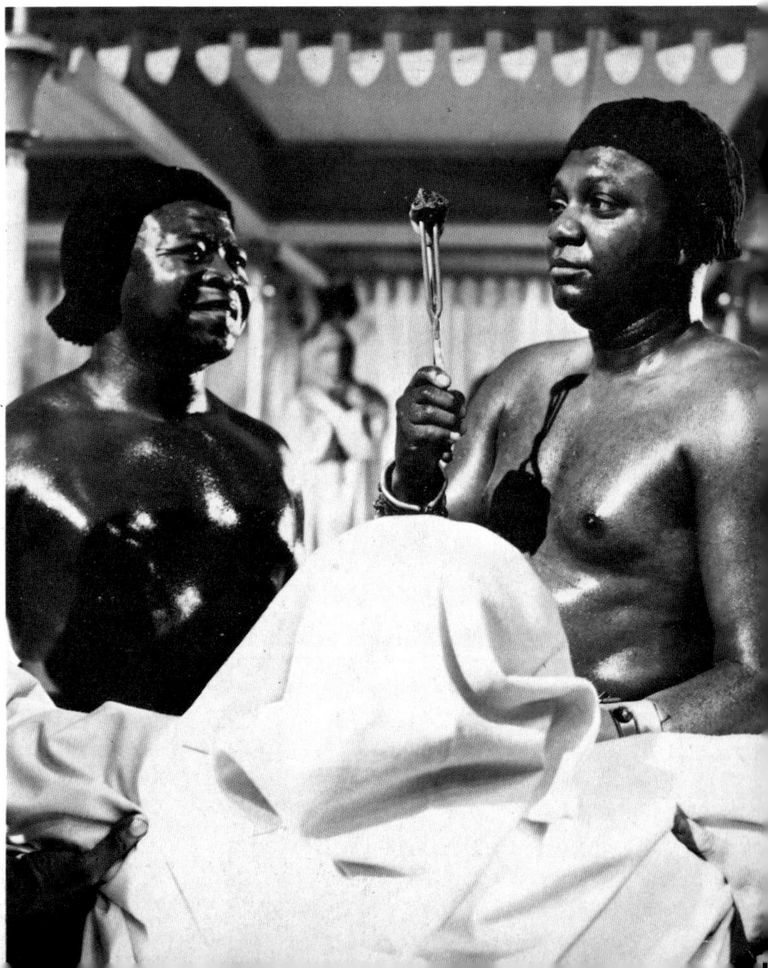

and spears thrust through him, and is only diverted by the appearance of Banning's wife Isobel (Yvonne Furneaux), who is the reincarnation of Ananka. Although Mehemet commands Lee to kill Isobel, the speechless and tormented creature turns on him and kills him. Carrying the girl with him, Lee is finally cornered in a swamp by the pursuing police, townspeople and Cushing, and sinking under the slimy mud, he dies there.

Like Karloff before him, Lee was only to play the Mummy once, in the first and best of the Hammer Mummy cycle. The next film, *Curse of the Mummy's Tomb* and *The Mummy's Shroud*, suffered the same anaemia that had killed off the previous Mummy cycle.

The latest in Hammer's attempt to continue the mummy film was much more successful. Based on one of Bram Stoker's lesser-known novels, *Blood From The Mummy's Tomb* (GB 1971) packed new and more effective horror in the story of the avenging spirit of the ancient Egyptian Queen Tera's possession of a modern girl. An archaeological expedition led by Professor Fuchs (Andrew Keir) breaks into the tomb where they find the preserved corpse of Queen Tera, surrounded by the relics placed there by the entombing priests. Severed by the priests, her hand, bearing the ruby ring which was the source of her power, still bleeds. Professor Fuchs brings the body and relics to England where his wife has died giving birth to their daughter Margaret at the exact moment of the opening of the tomb. On her twenty-first birthday, Fuchs gives his daughter the ring taken from the hand of Tera. Gradually Margaret becomes possessed by Tera's evil spirit, rejecting her boyfriend Tod Browning in favour of help from Corbeck, a member of her father's expedition. Tera embarks upon an orgy of terror and destruction as her spirit visits each member of the expedition, bringing about their violent deaths as she recovers the relics in their possession. Tera/Margaret (Valerie Leon) wills Tod's death and, as Corbeck tries to revive the body of Tera by reading from the Scroll of Life, the film reaches a macabre and powerful climax as Professor Fuchs interrupts the ceremony and manages to mutilate Tera's corpse, unleashing forces which bring the whole building crashing down upon them. But, in a fine last scene, the sole survivor of the destruction, swathed in bandages, is seen in hospital—it is Margaret, 'mummified' by the very hospital treatment that has saved her life! The film is full of fine horror effects and strange perverse shocks, and the still-bleeding hand, with the stigma of the huge ruby ring, is an image redolent with terror.

Scenes from Terence Fisher's The Mummy *(Hammer 1959). As punishment for the desecration of the tomb of Princess Ananka, Christopher Lee* (facing page) *has his tongue cut out. Christopher Lee breaks Felix Aylmer's neck* (below left)*, and, after bullets have failed to stop the mummy, Peter Cushing plunges a spear into the creature from the dead* (below right).

ABOVE *Andrea King gazes with terror on the living severed hand in Robert Florey's* The Beast with Five Fingers *(WB 1947).*
TOP LEFT *Boris Karloff leads the expedition, plagued by carnivorous plants and zombies, in* Voodoo Island *(Bel-Air 1957).*
TOP RIGHT *The Knights Templar rise from the dead to terrify the heroine in* Tombs of the Blind Dead *(Plata Films/Interfilme 1972).*
RIGHT *Dickie Owen as the Mummy carries the unconscious Jeanne Roland through the sewers in* The Curse of the Mummy's Tomb *(Hammer-Swallow 1964).*

First cousin to the mummy in horror films is the zombie, a revived corpse with no soul, animated by the power of voodoo. The classic German horror film *Das Kabinett des Dr. Caligari* (*The Cabinet of Dr. Caligari*) (Germany 1920), which remains a landmark in screen terror, gave the cinema its first zombie in the flitting black-clad figure of the 'undead' Conrad Veidt.

Dr. Caligari (Werner Krauss) is a travelling hypnotist who has under his control the 'somnambulist' Cesare (Conrad Veidt). Caligari is finally allowed to exhibit his 'creature' at the Holstenwall fair, but not before the doctor has been humiliated by the town clerk from whom he has sought permission. That night the clerk is murdered in his room by Cesare, controlled by the will of Caligari. The following day Jane (Lil Dagover) is taken to the fair by two young men, Francis (who also tells the story) and Alan. They enter Caligari's booth and question the briefly awakened Cesare about the future. Foolishly asking how long he will live, Alan is chilled to be told 'Until dawn!' Cesare keeps his word, killing Alan that night under Caligari's influence.

Suspecting that the murders are Cesare's work, Francis tries to prove it. In the meanwhile, Caligari sends his zombie to kill Jane, but faced with the beauty of the sleeping girl, Cesare is unable to murder her. Instead he kidnaps her and in a sequence still as powerful today, he flees with her in his arms over contorted rooftops and through painted streets with impossible perspectives. Trapped by the pursuing villagers, Cesare dies. Confronting Dr. Sonnow, head of the local insane asylum, with the corpse of Cesare, Francis exposes him as Dr. Caligari. Obsessed to the point of madness by the legend of a mediaeval sorcerer who travelled through Europe with a somnambulist under his control, Caligari had been emulating the exploits of his eleventh-century model. The original script ended at this point with the completion of Francis' narrative, but Lang filmed a prologue and epilogue set in the gardens of what turned out to be an asylum, so that the story told by Francis was turned into the figment of a diseased mind. Needless to say, this 'framing device' was inserted by Lang very much against the original authors' wishes!

The film became and has remained a milestone in the cinema and in the horror film in particular. With its slinking, leotard-clad 'somnambulist', the bizarre and unnerving perspectives of its sets, the film was hailed as a classic throughout the world.

Bela Lugosi created some of the most convincing 'undead' in *White Zombie*. As Murder Legendre, Lugosi reanimated corpses through voodoo to create cheap silent labour for Haiti's sugar mills, always hard at work even when one of their number was ground up with the sugar! Lugosi took the role of Legendre and played it for all it was worth, in sombre dress, eyes alive with evil and with an accompanying 'familiar'—a vulture—and an ever-present bodyguard of six hideous zombies. His truly satanic presence transcended the film's poor sound recording, quick shooting schedule and generally scrimped budget, to permeate every scene, aided by atmospheric photography by Arthur Martinelli and a haunting musical arrangement of the negro spiritual *Listen To The Lambs*.

ABOVE *The dead arise.* Tombs of the Blind Dead *(Plata Films/Interfilme 1972).*
ABOVE RIGHT *Dead end. Roddy McDowell's mummified mother from* It *(Goldstar 1966), and, back to life, the Golem carries the unconscious Jill Hayworth* (right).

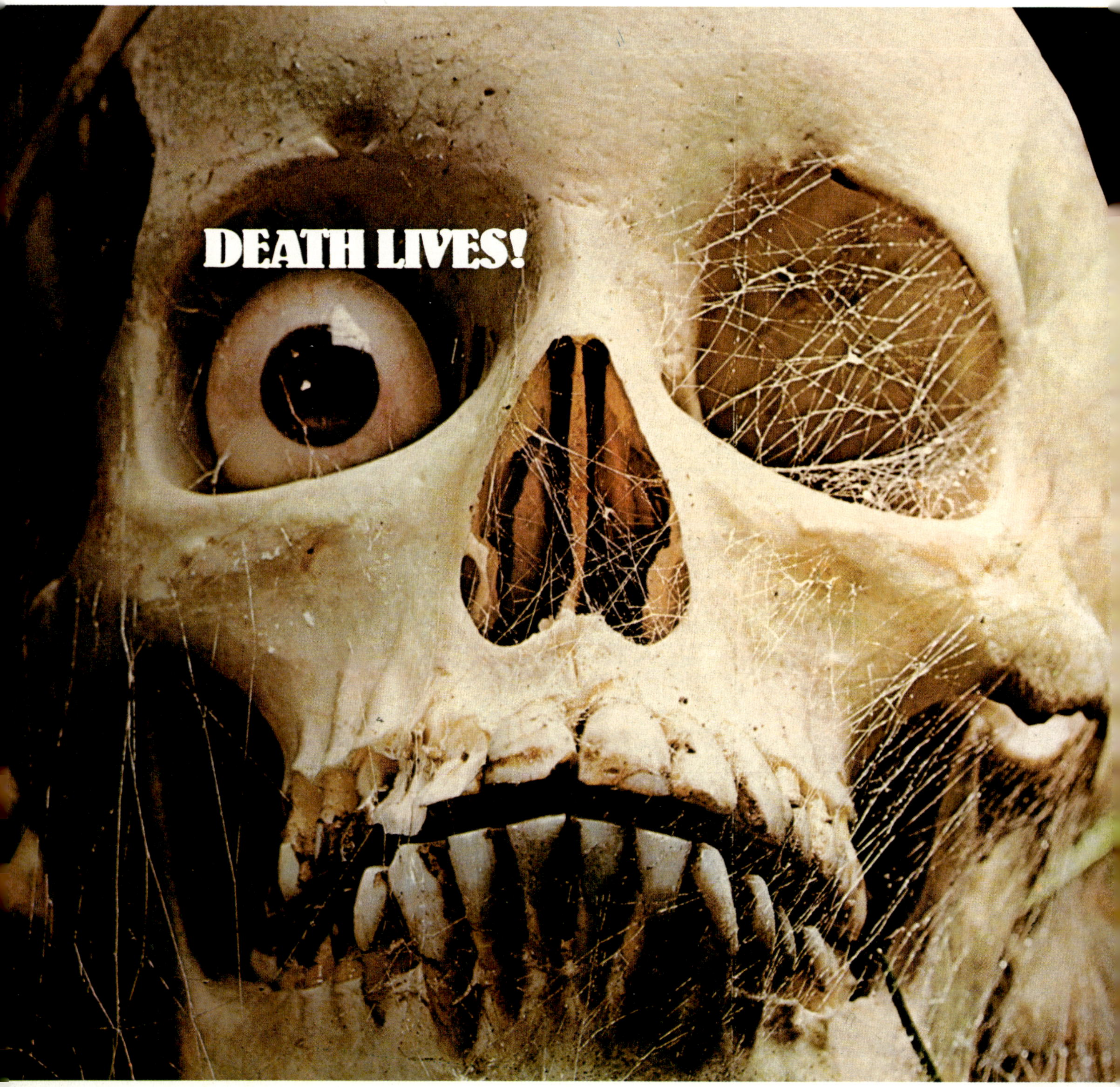
DEATH LIVES!

Take five startling tales of horror created by the publisher of Mad Magazine, have them whipped up by the producers of "The House That Dripped Blood," directed by one of the top suspense directors, played by a distinguished cast headed by Sir Ralph Richardson, Joan Collins, Peter Cushing, Ian Hendry, Richard Greene, Patrick Magee and Nigel Patrick. That's the formula for a new peak in horror-suspense for both the mass and class audience.

Metromedia Producers Corporation presents An Amicus Production "Tales From The Crypt" starring Joan Collins, Peter Cushing, Roy Dotrice, Richard Greene, Ian Hendry, Patrick Magee, Barbara Murray, Nigel Patrick, Robin Phillips and Sir Ralph Richardson. Screenplay by Milton Subotsky, produced by Max J. Rosenberg and Milton Subotsky, executive producer Charles Fries, directed by Freddie Francis, distributed by Cinerama Releasing.

"TALES FROM THE CRYPT"

THE VAULT OF HORROR

Madeline (Madge Bellamy) sails to Haiti to marry Neil in Port-au-Prince but is persuaded on board ship by wealthy plantation owner Charles Beaumont (Robert Fraser) to have the wedding on his estate. Beaumont, who wants Madeline for himself, enlists the aid of Murder Legendre to prevent the marriage. Horror is generated from the very beginning, as Madeline and her fiancé are halted in their carriage by chanting Haitians burying one of their dead at the crossroads, while along the skyline moves a column of zombies on their way to labour. Later, as the wedding banquet proceeds, in a scene of mounting horror, Legendre stands in the shadows fashioning a doll of wax to represent Madeline. As he melts it, so the bride collapses, apparently dead. Beaumont and Legendre abduct the girl's corpse with the aid of Legendre's zombie bodyguard and the film reaches heights of palpable horror with scenes of the undead Madeline moving like a wraith through the endless passages of Legendre's castle. The horror even transcends the melodramatic climax which sends Beaumont with the evil Legendre and his voodoo entourage plunging over the castle ramparts to their death on the rocks below. Released from the voodoo spell, Madeline is reunited with Neil.

White Zombie is a minor masterpiece of horror, fluidly cinematic and with a performance from Lugosi that for some is greater than his *Dracula*.

In 1943, Val Lewton produced *I Walked With A Zombie* for RKO. The title came from a series of newspaper stories dealing with voodoo in Haiti, but the script for the film took its substance from *Jane Eyre*. Although rushed on production time and budget, Lewton and his director, Jacques Tourneur fashioned a film full of terror, especially in the key sequence when the nurse (Frances Dee) and her catatonic charge Jessica (Christine Gordon) walk through the cane fields at night towards the menacing drums of the voodoo celebrants. The nurse finally discovers that her charge is not just ill but is actually one of the living dead, created by voodoo only to be destroyed again by the same evil forces. The restrained horror of the film and its climactic shocks make the film arguably the most horrific of the voodoo cycle: perhaps what it lacks is the central power of a Lugosi to add a deeper dimension of terror.

Lugosi starred in a deteriorating sequence of zombie films with little horror or merit. *Valley of The Zombies* (US 1946) plumbed the depths, and it was left for Dean Martin and Jerry Lewis in *Scared Stiff* (US 1953) to attempt to give the undead what Abott and Costello had given to practically every other monster!

Roger Corman brought some style back to the undead in *Tales of Horror* (1962) when, in the episode *The Case of M. Valdemar*, Basil Rathbone hypnotized Vincent Price at the point of death, to keep him between life and death for months. Finally, in a genuinely horrific sequence, Price rises from death to envelop the evil Rathbone. Rathbone dies of terror and, released from his hypnotic spell, Price literally liquefies over him in a truly shocking scene. For once, the publicists, armed with horror beyond their description, left the scene to be described by its original author, Edgar Allen Poe: '. . . and there was an oozing liquid putrescence . . . all that remained of M. Valdemar'!

Hammer made their one foray into zombie country with *Plague of the Zombies* (1966). Making horrific use of colour, the story is that of a squire who creates a zombie workforce to work his tin mine in Cornwall. The zombies are finally destroyed in an all-purpose fire and explosion in the mine, but not before the film has supplied some real moments of terror: the nightmarish green vision of the dead rising, with the graveyard earth heaving in waves as fingers and hands scrabble their way out of the grave, and the beheading of the unlucky Alice, in order to save her from zombiehood. The film, in its own modest way, managed to create and sustain a mood of terror.

The low budget horror film *Night of the Living Dead* (1969) showed that the genre had lost none of its power to shock. In a world overrun by zombies revived by radiation from a rocket abortively fired at Venus, a group of survivors battle against the ravaging undead with fire as they find themselves trapped in a house. An escape plan fails, resulting in the death of a young couple who had taken refuge in the house, and the hero, Ben, finds himself barricaded in the basement, as the rest of the house is taken by fresh hordes of zombies. Unaware that squads of armed men are now eliminating the zombies, which can be killed by a bullet or blow to the head, Ben hears the shooting and, believing rescue to be near, emerges only to be shot as a zombie. Despite the all too obvious limitations of the film, *Night of the Living Dead* never lost the momentum of terror started by the first zombie attack in a country churchyard.

LEFT *Joe Cornelius played the subterranean monster, seen here at bay, in Freddie Francis'* Trog *(Herman Cohen 1970).*

ABOVE *A zombie attacks the Cornish vicar (Roy Royston) in* Plague of the Zombies *(Hammer 1967).*
RIGHT *Peter Cushing rises from the grave in an award winning performance as Grimsdyke in* Tales From The Crypt *(Metromedia/Amicus 1971).*

Zombies are among the few screen horrors never to have met their nemesis at the hands of comedians. In a remake of Paul Leni's 1927 version of *The Cat and The Canary* (itself remade in sound in 1930 and retitled *The Cat Creeps*) Bob Hope and Paulette Goddard, with not a little sinister effect added by Gale Sondergaard and a zombie thrown in for good measure, made a delightful assault on the genre in *The Ghost Breakers* (US 1940). But the undead are unlikely to be kept down even by something as sharp and potent as Bob Hope's wit, and will no doubt continue to shock and terrify in years to come!

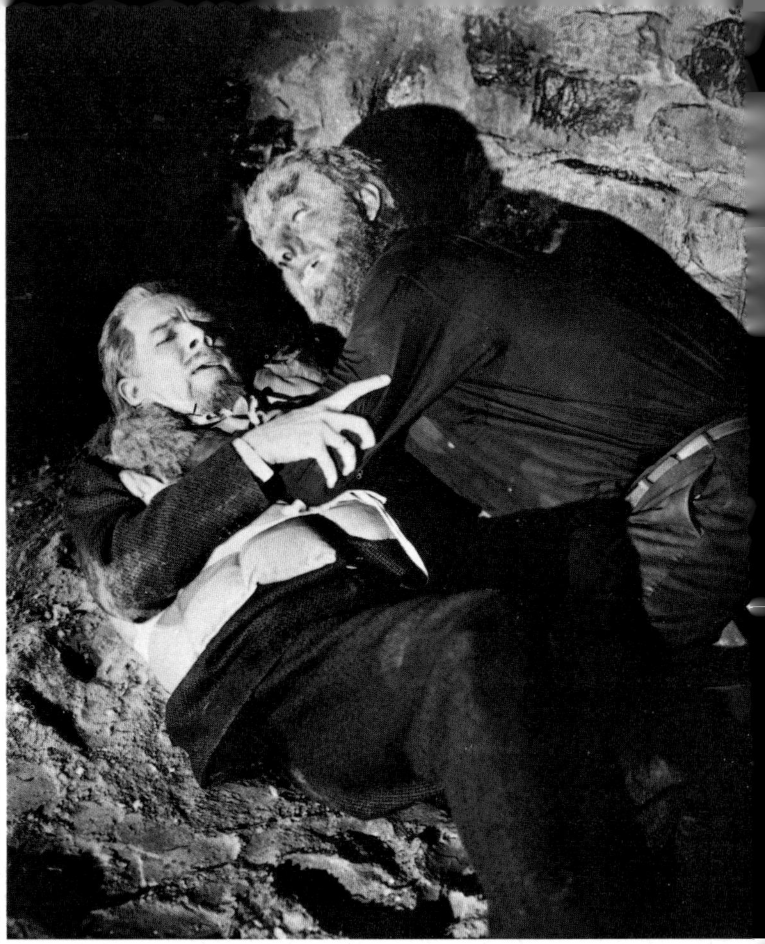
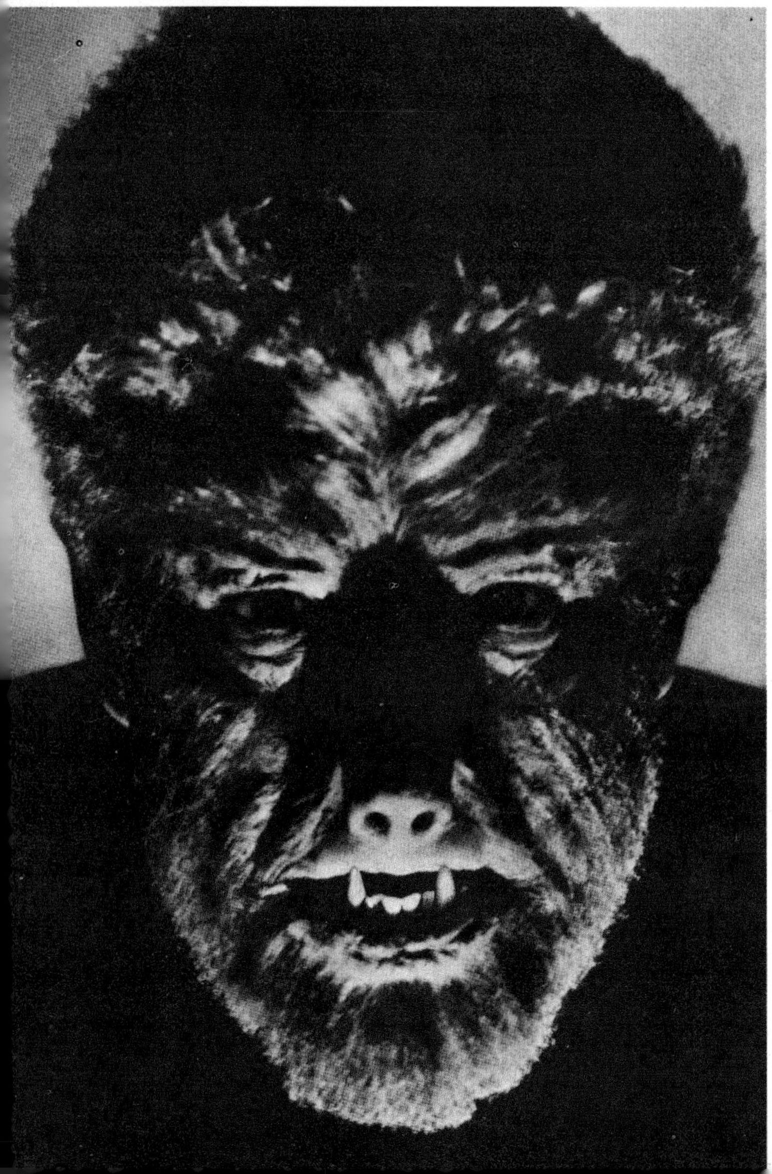

METAMORPHOSES & MASQUERADES

"Even a man who is pure in heart and says his prayers by night,
Can become a wolf when the wolfbane blooms and the autumn moon is bright."
Ancient gypsy proverb in The Wolf Man

THE MOST frequently recurring screen monster after the vampire—the werewolf—has its origins in various Central European and other mythologies, and probably, in the horror and fear generated by rabies. But while Pliny, Plato, Petronius all mention *lycanthropy*, the screen has had to develop its own legends about the men who turn into raving beasts when the moon is full.

After Karloff and Lugosi's monstrous successes, Carl Laemmle of Universal Pictures decided to create another monster. In *Werewolf of London* (US 1935), Laemmle and make-up artist Jack Pierce attempted to turn Henry Hull not only into a werewolf but also into another horror star. They succeeded in their first aim but not in the second.

Hull played an English botanist, Wilfred Glendon, who is bitten by a werewolf, Dr. Yogami (Warner Oland), while searching in Tibet for the exotic flower, *Marifasa Lupina*, which blooms only in the moonlight. Back in London with the flower, Glendon himself becomes a werewolf at the full moon, savagely killing a woman. Dr. Yogami returns to inform Glendon that the only cure for his lycanthropy is the Marifasa flower. Meanwhile, a plague of brutal killings terrorizes London and it soon becomes obvious that not one but two werewolves are loose in the stricken city. Dr. Yogami, after taking the mystic flower, reveals himself as the other wolf man and is killed by Glendon. Because the werewolf 'instinctively seeks to kill the thing it loves best', Glendon attacks his wife (Valerie Hobson), but is shot by the police. At death he changes back from wolf to man.

Neither Hull nor the werewolf, full of self-pity, was particularly successful. Refusing to submit to the full treatment, Hull forced the make-up man to devise a relatively un-hairy make-up which, although it took some four hours to apply and a further two to remove, proved insufficiently bestial. More effective were John P. Fulton's special effects transforming Hull into the wolf-man in a series of precise double exposures.

Having failed to create either a new monster or a new horror star, Universal waited six years until, with *The Wolf Man* (1941) they found their new monster and their new star in Lon Chaney Junior, whose father, Lon Chaney Senior, had been the first Universal horror star. The Wolf Man became Chaney's creation for all time, as much as Frankenstein's monster was Karloff's.

Chaney played Lawrence Stewart Talbot, heir to the noble estates of Sir John Talbot (Claude Rains). Bitten by a werewolf (Bela Lugosi), Talbot himself becomes infected. He finds himself unwillingly condemned to change into a wolf and kill for all eternity, a fate explained to him by the strange gypsy fortune teller Maliva (Maria Ouspenskaya), Lugosi's mother. Nobody will believe Talbot's wild story and the murders continue until his father manages to kill him by smashing his head in with a silver tipped cane.

With a very strange Hollywood version of Wales, the fine acting by all the film's principals, plus superb make-up by Jack Pierce, involving a rubber nose piece, yak hairs, and a six-hour session in the make-up chair, with a further twenty-two hours to film the metamorphosis from man to wolf —*The Wolf Man* established itself as the definitive werewolf film. For Lon Chaney, destined to play the eventually doomed and tragic Lawrence Talbot until he met Abbott and Costello, the creation was his personal triumph, making all the agonies required for the transformation scenes worth every painful minute. Curt Siodmak's literate script established new monstrous 'traditions', notably the 'law' that the bite of a werewolf turned the bitten one into another doomed to eternal life of murder at the full moon, and that the creature could only be killed by a silver bullet or by a stick covered with silver.

TOP LEFT *Lon Chaney Jnr., the perfect werewolf, menaces super-screamer Evelyn Ankers in* The Wolf Man *(Universal 1941).*
TOP RIGHT *Lon Chaney Jnr. back again in his yak hairs in* House of Dracula *(Universal 1945).*
FAR LEFT *The unstoppable and unshaven Lon Chaney Jnr. as* The Wolf Man *(Universal 1941).*
LEFT *Henry Hull in Jack Pierce's unique make-up in* Werewolf of London *(Universal 1935)*

ABOVE *Michael Landon plays Whit Bissell's title creation,* I Was a Teenage Werewolf *(AIP 1957)*

Chaney was back again as Lawrence Talbot in *Frankenstein Meets the Wolf Man* (US 1943) a film designed to provide the battle of the century for the two great Universal monsters. Lon Chaney finally essayed the role of the Frankenstein monster for this film, which climaxed with the two monsters in a savage fight to the death, destroying Frankenstein's laboratory before they are themselves destroyed as villagers dynamite a dam to flood the laboratory.

In the *House of Frankenstein* (1944) the drowned Chaney is thawed out from a block of ice by Karloff. Doomed once more to immortal lycanthropy, Chaney is far from grateful, but, after falling in love with Elena Verdugo, he is finally laid to rest again after she shoots him as he changes to wolf man at full moon. The 'silver bullet' fired by the hand of one who loves him', proved strong enough only to keep Talbot down among the dead until 1945 when he turned up alive and in jail for *The House of Dracula*. Talbot is taken from jail to the castle laboratory of Dr. Franz Edelman (Onslow Stevens), who diagnoses his lycanthropy: 'His glands generate certain hormones which bring about the physical changes. There is a crowding of the brain because the cranial cavity failed to enlarge sufficiently.' His amazing diagnosis proves correct and, after enlarging Talbot's cranial cavity with a special bone-softening mould, the wolf-man is cured and even gets the girl!

However, his peace is disturbed once more, and, changing into the wolf man in the middle of a fancy-dress ball, Lawrence Talbot saves Lou Costello from a brain transplant, only to plunge to his death in the sea, taking Dracula with him, in *Abbott and Costello Meet Frankenstein* (1948).

The werewolf survived Chaney in many forms and in many countries. Whit Bissell, fresh from his triumphs in creating the Teenage Frankenstein, helped producer Herman Cohen turn an investment of only 150,000 dollars into a profit of nearly two and a half million dollars, a far more striking metamorphosis than that featured in *I Was a Teenage Werewolf* (1957)! But once again Hammer films, with their colour remake *The Curse of the Werewolf* (1961) from Guy Endore's famous novel *The Werewolf of Paris*, infused fresh blood into the genre.

Disregarding the book's original setting or their own location in England, *The Curse of The Werewolf* was set in eighteenth-century Spain. The werewolf of the title was the child of a beggar incarcerated for years in the dungeons of Castillo Siniestro, having offended the cruel Marquis on his wedding night. As the years passed the beggar gradually became more animal than human and finally dies from the exertion of raping a mute servant girl thrown into his cell for having displeased the Marquis. The girl escapes, murdering the marquis, to find sanctuary in the home of Professor Carido (Clifford Evans) until she dies giving birth to a son, Leon.

An intimation of the greater horrors to come takes place when, as the child is about to be baptized, the holy water in the font boils over.

Adopted by the Professor, Leon is revealed at the age of six to be a werewolf when shepherds fire at a wolf attacking their flocks and the boy returns home in the morning, bleeding from the buckshot in him. The village priest tells the Professor that only love can overcome the curse of the werewolf and this proves the case, with Leon reaching manhood unaware of his affliction.

When Christina (Catherine Feller) rejects him, the adult Leon (Oliver Reed) finally succumbs again, embarking in werewolf form on a rampage of brutal killings. In an attempt to help him, the professor chains Leon but he has the strength to break the bonds and flee once more. Now even Christina's love is insufficient to effect a cure. Breaking out of the local jail where he has been held for murder, Leon changes into the wolf man and,

ABOVE *Jean Marais and Josette Day in Jean Cocteau's* La Belle et La Bête *(André Paulve 1946).*

pursued in true tradition by the villagers, he calls to his stepfather for release as he stands trapped on the rooftops of the village. At the top of the church tower, Leon finds peace as he dies from a bullet forged from a silver crucifix fired by his compassionate stepfather.

Directed by Terence Fisher, screenplay by John Elder (Anthony Hinds), Bernard Robinson's evocative sets and the effective werewolf make-up combined with fine performances from Oliver Reed, Clifford Evans and Richard Wordsworth as the beggar, to produce a really frightening horror film. Terror comes early to the film in the character of the Marquis (Anthony Dawson), and is sustained by the degradation of the beggar into something bestial. More horror is unleashed in the portrayal of six-year-old Leon by Justin Walters, palms covered with thick black hair, teeth bared and feral, and eyes blazing red as he screams at the full moon.

Oliver Reed gave the adult Leon the full power of his good looks and fine physique, contrasting with the werewolf's cover of matted silvery hair, blood-suffused eyes and bared fangs. He was able to inspire sheer terror as the creature while suggesting Leon's tragic knowledge that within him he carried the seeds of his own destruction. The final scene when, cornered by the villagers, he begs for death from the Professor, combines both effective pathos and horror.

Having literally cut his teeth on Hammer horror roles Reed abandoned horror to become an international film star. 'Rather than risk forever being tagged "The Hammer Horror Star",' he says, 'I left Hammer and struggled for a period.'

While the werewolf usually has no control over his unfortunate metamorphoses, the same cannot be said of the changes brought about by Dr. Jekyll and his alter ego, Mr. Hyde. His many screen appearances from 1908 onwards make it quite clear that the schizophrenic hero consistently brings trouble down on his own head! However, Dr. Jekyll himself played by Fredric March, has explained his self-imposed changes addressing his students in the 1931 version of the film. 'I shall not,' he tells his audience of students, 'dwell today on the human body, in sickness and in health; today I want to talk to you of a greater marvel: the soul of Man. My analysis of this Soul—the human psyche leads me to believe that man is not truly one . . . but truly two. One of him strives for the nobilities of life; this we call his good self. The other seeks an expression of impulses that binds him with some dim animal relation with the earth; this we may call the bad. . . . Now, if these two selves could be separated from each other, how much better the good in us might be, what heights it might scale;

ABOVE and BELOW *Horror's only Oscar-winning performance—Fredric March in Rouben Mamoulian's* Dr. Jekyll and Mr. Hyde *(Paramount 1932).*
FACING PAGE *A new twist on the theme, Paul Massie plays the bearded Dr. Jekyll and the handsome, debonair Mr. Hyde in Terence Fisher's* The Two Faces of Dr. Jekyll *(Hammer 1960).*

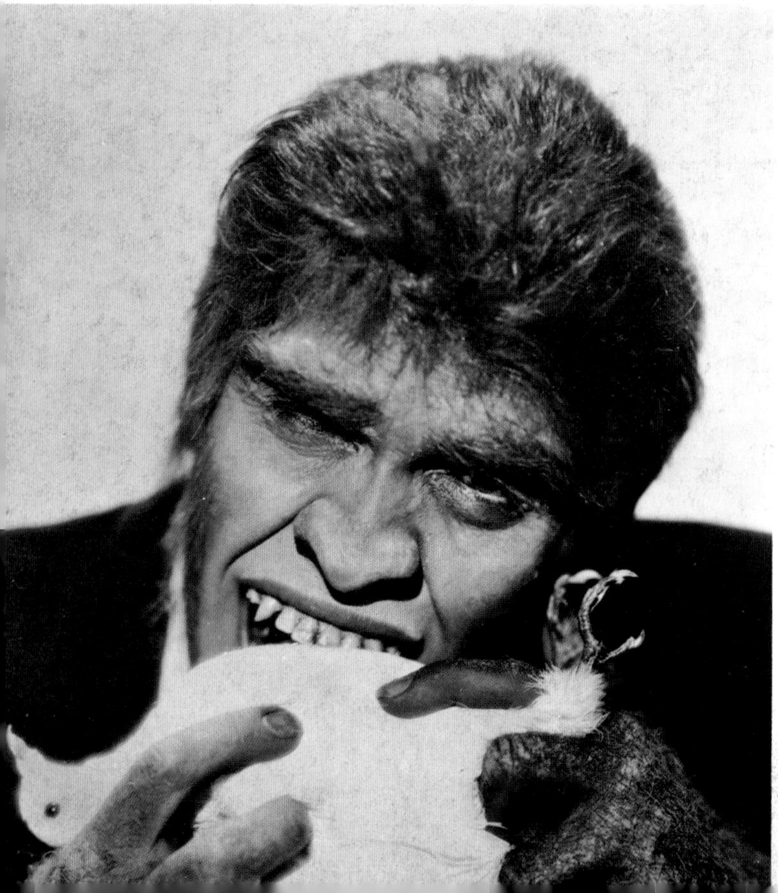

and the so-called evil, once liberated, would fulfil itself and trouble us no more.' Thus Dr. Jekyll describes the lofty motives which drive him to experiment with his dual nature, always with the same horrifying results.

The first film version was an American one made in 1908 by Colonel William Selig, who filmed all four acts of the Richard Mansfield stage play in one reel! The film opened, like the play, with the curtain rising, and Jekyll's first transformation occurs in the vicar's garden as he pays court to the cleric's daugher, Alice. Changing from 'the admirable gentleman and scholar to the ferocious brute of a maniac', Hyde attacks the girl, kills her father and vanishes to reappear as the admirable Dr. Jekyll once more.

The 'classic' silent *Dr. Jekyll and Mr. Hyde* was the John Barrymore portrayal made in 1920. The story was changed, to include not only Lord Henry from Oscar Wilde's *The Picture of Dorian Gray* but also seductive dancer and star discovery, Nita Naldi. But the picture was Barrymore's, who gave a brilliant portrayal in the dual role, in the early stages of transformation 'dislocating' and contorting his classic features to become the brutish Hyde, relying little on make-up or camera tricks. Barrymore was to give horror films prestige with one reviewer writing of the film when it opened in New York: 'One leaves the theatre with the belief that motion pictures are on the verge of a new era.'

Fredric March played *Dr. Jekyll and Mr. Hyde* in the first sound version of the story, winning himself an Academy Award in the process—the only screen monster ever to do so! Director Rouben Mamoulian achieved a notable impact in horror with his transformation of the handsome matinee idol March into the simian and revolting Mr. Hyde. For March it meant weeks of arriving at the studios at 6 a.m. so that make-up man Wally Westmore could 'spend four hours building pieces on my nose and cheeks, sticking fangs in my mouth, and pushing cotton-wool up my nostrils!' The hideous transformation was accomplished in one take, without superimposition; this was achieved by building up on March's 'normal' face the complete Hyde creation, layer by layer, each coat of make-up in a different colour, and gradually becoming more detailed than the previous layer. Finally, the metamorphosis was achieved by holding various colour filters in front of the camera lens: as each filter was removed, it exposed a different layer of the multicoloured make-up until Jekyll had become Hyde in one single, fluid and very frightening take.

Mamoulian had already used the subjective

camera to great effect at the beginning of the film where we, the audience, were Dr. Jekyll, playing the organ, leaving the house and entering a carriage to be driven along to the university, jostled among the students until, with a complete revolution of the camera, we are at the back of the auditorium, no longer the doctor but looking at him from among his students as he addresses them. His use of the subjective camera again when Jekyll drinks the potion is a tour de force. We become Jekyll again, the laboratory spinning around us, while incredible sound effects—the beating of Mamoulian's own heart, the tampered-with beating of a gong—all come together to 'transform' the audience as well as Jekyll. The camera stops spinning, the sound diminishes to laboured breathing, as we survey the laboratory. The camera gradually nears a mirror until, after an infinity, we see Hyde, a horror that is not a let-down after all the preceding events.

Not only is Jekyll/Hyde a figure of horror, but his activities too bring with them their fair share of terror, particularly in the murder of the prostitute 'Champagne' (Miriam Hopkins), horror made all the more scaring for being explicit as the girl, forced to sing by Hyde, stops abruptly as Hyde bends over her, out of camera. The silence before Hyde rises again is almost unendurable.

March's performance in both roles fully justified his Academy Award, and this film, the only essay in horror by its star or director remains far and away the finest film of *Dr. Jekyll and Mr. Hyde.*

The 1941 remake, with Spencer Tracy and Ingrid Bergman was a distinct let-down. Made with all the production values that Metro-Goldwyn-Mayer could muster, director Victor Fleming made a film that was slow, boring in parts, with a Hyde who, changing on a montage, relied less on expert make-up than a sneering expression that repelled rather than horrified. Only Ingrid Bergman came out of the film with triumph, in her performance as the prostitute Ivy.

For once, Hammer's three attempts at the cycle totally misfired. The first, a comic spoof of the Jekyll/Hyde story had Bernard Bresslaw as *The Ugly Duckling* (1959), a moronic descendant of the original Doctor Jekyll rediscovering the mystic potion and changing himself into debonair and daring Teddy Hyde, lover and gang leader. The film was as dire as its Abbott and Costello predecessors had been. Hammer ventured again, this time in colour, with *The Two Faces of Dr. Jekyll* (1960). Script writer Wolf Mankowitz attempted to give the familiar plot a new twist by making the

evil Hyde clean shaven, handsome and sexually irresistible, with his other self the morose bearded scientist. Paul Massie played the lead but, despite the presence of Christopher Lee and the usual careful Hammer production values, the film failed to horrify.

A comic version of the story which worked, and which gave a certain amount of genuine scares in the transformation scene was Jerry Lewis' *The Nutty Professor* (1963). After that, the double doctor lay dormant until *I Monster* (1970) starring Christopher Lee as Jekyll and Peter Cushing as his friend Utterson.

Despite its stars and its producers' claim that it was the most faithful screen adaptation of Stevenson's book, the film is not a success, partly due to a 3D process that never came off.

The most recent version of the story *Dr. Jekyll and Sister Hyde* (1971), had Hammer making another stab at the Doctor, this time eliminating the need for special effects by making the 'Hyde' character a woman, Sister Hyde, who murders a series of women in order to assist Dr. Jekyll in his search for the 'elixir of life'. Despite its plot gimmick, with Ralph Bates playing Henry Jekyll and Martine Beswick as Sister Hyde, the film never did find the elixir of life.

Transformation of yet another kind provided a short genre of films of which the first made a star of its leading actor, Claude Rains, despite the fact that his face was seen only momentarily in death. The film was Universal's *The Invisible Man* (1933), directed by the man who had made Universal's *Frankenstein*, James Whale. Karloff had turned down the lead since it required only a speaking voice and a final shot of the actor's face and he felt that it would be a film for the special effects men. As it was, it was left to Rains to deliver some of the best mad scientist dialogue ever spoken in a horror film, including the memorable 'We'll start with a few murders. Big men. Little men. Just to show we make no distinction!'

Rains, appearing throughout the film, except in death, gloved, bandaged and wearing dark glasses, played Dr. Griffin, a scientist who had discovered that the Indian drug monocaine, when injected under the skin, made flesh and blood invisible. Not knowing that the drug has side effects which will drive him insane the bandaged Dr. Griffin descends on the English village of Ipping, renting a room at the inn. Villagers, uneasy at his appearance, are terrified when, confronted by the village constable, Griffin undoes his bandages, sheds his clothes and disappears! Forced to confide his plight, Griffin in a state of megalomania induced by the drug, tells his horrified colleague, Dr. Kemp (William Harrigan) of his plans for world domination. 'Power,' he cries, 'to make the world grovel at my feet, to walk into the gold vaults of nations, the chambers of kings, into the holy of holies. Even the moon is frightened of me, frightened to death! The whole world is frightened to death!' Griffin escapes, beginning his reign of terror with robbery, murder and the derailing of a train. Kemp calls in the police but the Invisible Man eludes all attempts at capture until he is forced to take shelter in a barn during a snowstorm. The farmer, terrified by his discovery, reports to the police 'There's breathin' in me barn!' The barn is surrounded and, as his footprints appear in the snow, Griffin is shot, appearing at last in his moment of death.

In a script adapted from H. G. Wells' novel by R. C. Sherrif and Phillip Wylie, the film gave Rains and Whale free rein of which they and Universal's special effects expert, John P. Fulton, took full advantage. Whale's brand of quirky black humour which had for many marred his *Bride of Frankenstein*, was ideally suited to *The Invisible Man*. There was off-beat humour as Griffin explained the various problems required to maintain his invisibility—avoiding exposure for an hour after meals, keeping absolutely clean so as to avoid appearing as a dark outline, and keeping out of rain: 'It would make me shine like a bubble.' Whale even included a shot of the invisible Griffin happily singing 'Here we go gathering nuts in May!' disappearing as a pair of empty, dancing trousers. The humour contrasted well with Griffin's chilling madness as he outlined his terrible plans for world domination, and the film was a complete success.

Never a Studio to let a good monster die, in 1940 Universal brought Vincent Price to the screen in the title role of *The Invisible Man Returns*, only once more to pay in insanity for his invisibility as he sought to clear himself of the charge of killing his brother. Virginia Bruce became *The Invisible Woman* (1941), while Jon Hall became *The Invisible Agent* (1942) returning in 1944 to exact *The Invisible Man's Revenge*. The series was killed off finally in 1951 by Universal's universal solution for any screen monster: when Arthur Franz met his fate in *Abbott and Costello Meet The Invisible Man*. Apart from a low-grade rash of 'Invisible Men' from Mexico and Argentina in the Sixties, the series was over.

In their infancy films were no more than just another fair-ground side-show, a modern 'freak' to

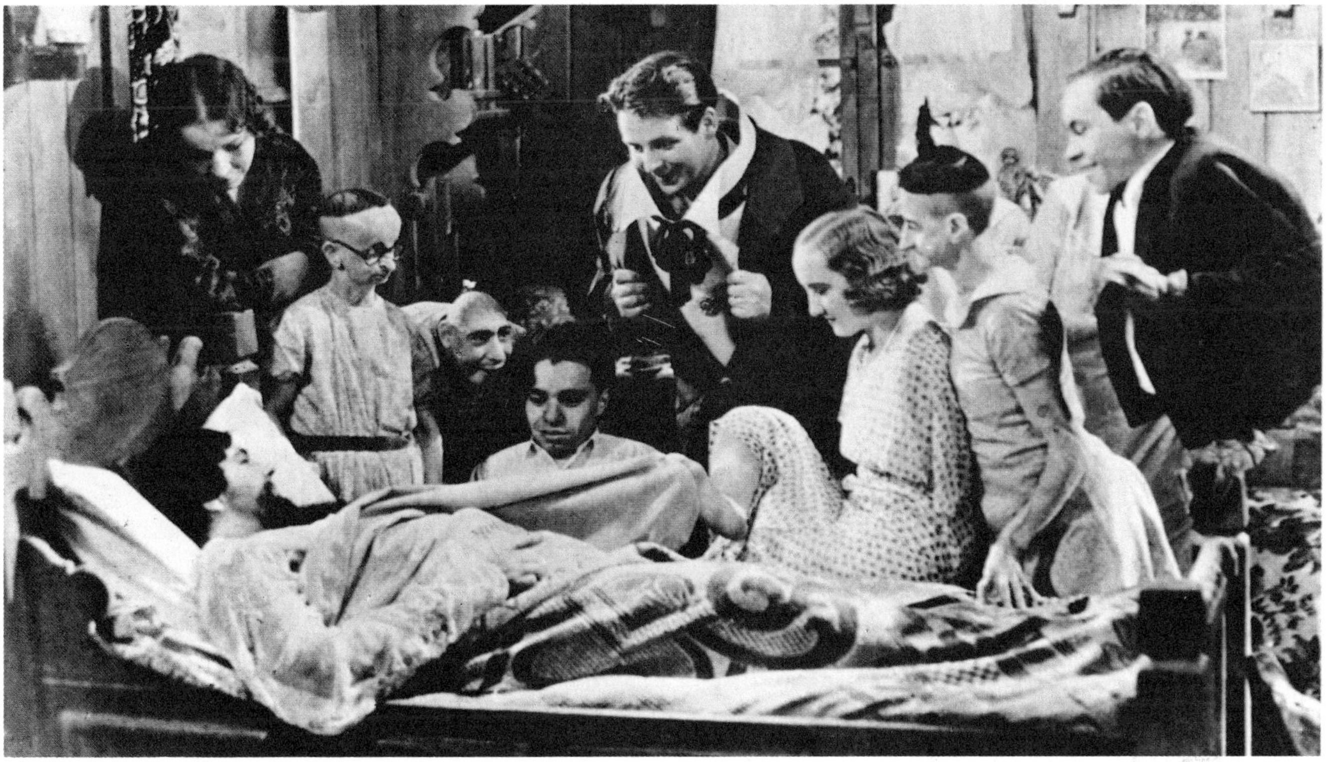

Tod Browning's over-horrifying use of real circus characters in Freaks *(Universal 1932).*

be viewed alongside all the other grotesques and 'monsters', real and masked, that made up the rest of the carnival.

The cinema produced only one horror film about freaks, Tod Browning's *Freaks* (US 1932), but it is perhaps the most disturbing and terrifying ever made. This exercise in the terror of the macabre was unique, being completely banned for thirty years by the British Censor, an event which may ultimately have contributed to much of its lurid fame. Loved by the midget Hans, the normal and beautiful trapeze artist Cleopatra (Olga Baclanova) leads him on, merely in cruel sport, until Cleopatra discovers that Hans has financial prospects. With the help of the strong man Hercules, her lover, she plans to marry the midget, later to kill him and get his money. At the wedding, however, attended by all the circus freaks, she is unable to conceal her revulsion for the grotesques, attempting to purge herself by taunting and humiliating Hans. Finally the freaks realize the truth and in one of the most horrifying sequences in the cinema, they turn on Cleopatra and Hercules, emasculating the strong man and, in a writhing, sliding, rain-soaked and an appalling scene of pure fright, the freaks overwhelm Cleopatra, slicing her into one of 'them', a hideous 'hen-woman' seen squatting in a bran pit in the final shot. The film, marred by stilted dialogue and excesses of melodrama, failed at the box-office, but the reason for its failure was much more basic than flawed film-making. Browning had used real circus people for his film-midgets, 'pinheads', giggling Siamese twins, a bearded lady and a human torso among others. The result was that the audiences were deprived of their one safety-valve in the cinema of horror, the innate knowledge of the screen monsters' off-screen 'reality'.

Lon Chaney Senior became the most famous of all screen monsters who used the mask of make-up to produce creatures of terror on the screen. With his many macabre portrayals he truly earned his title of 'Man of A Thousand Faces'—leading to the old joke (reputedly one that amused Chaney) of warning someone against crushing a spider, 'Don't step on it—it may be Lon Chaney!'

Born Alonso Chaney on April 1, 1883, in Colorado, he was the second son of deaf mute parents Frank and Emma Chaney. Born into a family where silence was the norm and mime and gesture the 'natural' way to communicate, Chaney finally left school for three years to tend his bedridden mother, 'telling' her in pantomime of the daily happenings and life in Colorado Springs. Out of necessity was born Chaney's mastery of mime, to which he added his near perfect use of make-up. His stardom in silent pictures was, in a sense, pre-ordained.

Before achieving horror stardom in *The Miracle Man* (1919) Chaney had appeared in over a hundred films, as extra and feature player, in an age when film-making was still, for the actor, very much a business of doing everything for himself, particularly creating 'characters' through make-up of his own devising. By 1913, after countless bit parts, mostly at Universal, Chaney received his first billing—indeed, he was the film's only named player!—in a comedy released by Universal called *Poor Jake's Demise*. He indicated his talent to terrify in *The Tragedy of Whispering Creek* in which he played The Greaser. Horror stardom came to him with his role as 'The Frog', a phoney cripple exploiting a blind faith healer in *The Miracle Man* (1919). In one single take he became 'cured' of his affliction, straightening from paralytic dislocation into an upright man again. This 'miracle' made audiences everywhere marvel at Chaney's change from grotesque to normal. Chaney himself had had some difficulty in deciding how to portray the grotesque Frog. 'In the first place,' he told an interviewer, 'I planned to be a cripple, have a withered hand, a hump on my back, but when I discovered that I had to unfold *twice* before the camera, these three infirmities were, of course impossible.' His final horrible make-up was arrived at after several sleepless nights. Chaney arrived at '. . . paralysis! I let my beard grow, and altogether I worked out a convincing make-up, horrible as it was.'

In the archetypal mad-scientist film, *A Blind Bargain* (1922) Chaney played the dual roles of the evil human experimenter, Dr. Lamb, and his hunchback assistant, part man, part ape, the result of a previous experiment.

1923 saw him back at Universal to play the hideous love-crazed hunchback Quasimodo in *The Hunchback of Notre Dame*. The story had already been filmed several times before, notably as *Notre Dame de Paris* (France 1911) and as *Esmeralda* (GB 1922) one of a series of *Tense Moments From Great Plays*, in which the title role was played by Sybil Thorndike and Quasimodo by Booth Conway. Chaney, horrific in a make-up which added another 70 pounds to his weight, turned in a performance that was a combined *tour de force* of acting and make-up, realizing perfectly the love and adoration of the hideous creature for the beautiful gypsy girl Esmeralda. His appearance matched that of Victor Hugo's imagination: described as looking like a human gargoyle, the hump-backed, twisted creature, one eye blind and bulging, sharp protruding teeth, jagged and uneven, a twisted nose and deformed cheekbones, he was 'an indefinable mixture of malice, bewilderment and sadness.' Chaney

LEFT *Vincent Price with Nan Gray in* The Invisible Man Returns *(Universal 1940).*
RIGHT *Charles Laughton in a brilliant performance as Quasimodo in William Dieterle's* The Hunchback of Notre Dame *(RKO Radio 1939).*

added a thirty-pound leather harness and forty pounds of rubber moulded into a hump and joined to the harness. Once in the rig, under a hideous hairy skin suit, he was unable to stand erect. The giant sets for the film included a life-size replica of the cathedral of Notre Dame. Working for the first time with Irving Thalberg, who was later to leave Universal and become the presiding genius at Metro-Goldwyn-Mayer, the film was a triumph as horror-spectacle, earning for Chaney world-wide acclaim and for the picture a place in the year's Ten Best Films.

However, the definitive screen Quasimodo belonged to Charles Laughton in the 1939 remake of *The Hunchback of Notre Dame*. Directed by William Dieterle, Laughton was able to project even more humanity in his performance while conveying only too vividly the horror of the creature. Even more than Chaney, Laughton stood out against the pure spectacle of the picture, where the people of Paris are paraded in nightmarish detail among the incredible sets by Van Nest Polglase. Transcending even Chaney's finest moments are the scenes in which Laughton, exuding sinister menace, is led through crowds, who shrink away as he turns the full horror of his appearance on them. Throughout the film, in scenes in the criminal underworld, peopled by deformed thieves and creatures of evil, the horror and tension are maintained, culminating in Quasimodo's final explosive orgy of destruction.

So great were his profits from *The Hunchback of Notre Dame*, Laemmle at Universal decided to film yet another Parisian horror story, this time an adaptation of Gaston Leroux's novel *The Phantom of the Opera*. They were forced to get Chaney back from MGM where he had made *He Who Gets Slapped* (1924) as the sadistically treated clown; a mad scientist horror role in *The Monster* (1924); and dual roles as Echo, the ventriloquist, who masquerades as *The Little Lady Who Sells Parrots* in Tod Browning's melodrama *The Unholy Three* (US 1925), achieving star status. This meant that for *The Phantom of The Opera*, Chaney, in probably his greatest horror creation, was able to make the film on his terms.

The film is a story of fairy-tale beginnings, with an unseen voice in the Paris Opera House coaching and admiring the young opera singer Christine, promising her stardom and escape from the chorus. Her tutor, whom Christine (Mary Philbin) calls the Spirit of Music is, in fact, the freak Erik, the 'Phantom of the Opera' who, feared by all the opera company, lives deep in the catacombs below the theatre, emerging on occasions to kill a stagehand

The grotesquely deformed Lon Chaney Snr. in the silent version of The Hunchback of Notre Dame *(Universal 1923).*

or to appear at a masqued Ball, suitably dressed as 'Death'. Living only for music, Erik tells Christine: 'Think only of your art and your master, for soon this spirit will take form and demand your love.'

The prima donna of the Opera falls ill, and Christine, singing in her place, is a great success. In spite of her obvious talent, the management replaces her with a better-known singer. The Phantom, determined to prove love for Christine, warns against her appearance, but when she does appear on stage, he brings the massive chandelier of the Opera House down upon the audience, whispering to the petrified management 'She sings to bring down the chandelier!' As panic rages through the theatre, the masked and cloaked Phantom appears and leads Christine through the dungeons, sewers and catacombs to his world below the Opera House. He sits down at the organ to play his own composition 'Don Juan Triumphant', preluding a scene of classic cinema and classic horror, Christine's unmasking of the Phantom. In a superb piece of montage, the tension builds up to a crescendo as the camera cuts from reaction shots of the girl's fearful face as she unmasks him, to Chaney, who suddenly swings to face the audience, a corroded, living skull. The director, Rupert Julian, piled on horror with a sequence of close shots, tilted shots and distorted views of this, the greatest of Chaney's creations, so that people screamed and fainted, a fact made much of by the studio publicity men.

After telling Christine to 'Feast your eyes, gloat your soul, on my accursed ugliness!' Erik allows her to leave to go back to the world outside, so long as she discloses nothing of what she has seen.

It is during the Masqued Ball that Christine, unaware of being spied upon from above the theatre roof by The Phantom, tells her suitor Raoul about Erik. She vanishes again, shortly afterwards, but Raoul, aided by the police, tracks the Phantom back to his underground den and the unfortunate Erik finally perishes at the hands of a mob, while Raoul and Christine are reunited.

There was great secrecy during the making of *The Phantom of The Opera*. No production stills of Chaney's make-up were released, and there were clashes between Chaney and director Rupert Julian, leading to another director, Edward Sedgwick being called in to complete the film, and Chaney directing himself in many scenes. There was considerable editing before the final version was released in September 1925, and while the film never entirely held together as an organic whole, its climactic moments of horror were some of the most powerful ever to be filmed. Colour was used to heighten scenes, particularly the Phantom's entrance as Edgar Allen Poe's 'Red Death' at the Masqued Ball, where the original two-colour Technicolor process was employed. In the ballet and opera sequences colour was also used and, particularly effective in adding sinister overtones to an already terrifying moment, Erik's swirling cape was hand-coloured for the scene where, unobserved, he clings to a statue of Apollo to overhear Christine tell Raoul of his secret existence.

But it was Chaney's make-up and its awful unmasking that was the keystone of horror. Chaney, in a daily ordeal of pain and disfigurement, had devised for himself a living skull, cadaverous, distorted and infinitely evil. It had its 'masked' counterpart in his appearance at the Ball as the Red Death, but there was nothing that could match the shock of its first appearance, made even more scaring by its revelation quite late in the film. To give his face the look of a skull, Chaney distended his nostrils with a wire clip which also served to lift the tip of his nose. He added rotting, jagged fangs to which he fixed small forks to draw back the corners of his mouth. His cheeks were distended by celluloid discs and cotton wool padding and he made his eyes bulge and dilate with chemical drops. Chaney was even able to make his unmasked appearance become progressively worse, until the final horror of the wild death ride as the mob pursues him in a coach through the streets of Paris and, ironically, past the still-standing set of Notre Dame Cathedral, the scene of his previous Universal horror triumph.

The Phantom of The Opera was remade again in 1943 by Universal, with Claude Rains in the title role, pursued by Nelson Eddy through the catacombs, while Terence Fisher directed Hammer's version (1962). This film, with Herbert Lom donning the mask of the Phantom, displayed atmospheric settings from Bernard Robinson and Don Mingaye, but neither remake came within striking distance of the true horror of Chaney's original.

Fay Wray, an actress who spent most of her time screaming as she was put upon in every conceivable way in horror films, was given the role of performing the horror screen's second greatest unmasking

Three different Phantoms of the Opera. Lon Chaney Snr. (top) *as the Red Death in the 1925 Universal silent production. Herbert Lom* (right) *gives Heather Sears a singing lesson in Hammer's 1962 colour version, and a masked Claude Rains* (far right) *from the Universal sound remake of 1943.*

in *The Mystery of The Wax Museum* (1933) made in the then new Technicolor process by Michael Curtiz. Lionel Atwill played Ivan Igor, confined to a wheelchair and without the use of his sculptor's hands after an insurance fire started by his partner had destroyed both his waxworks and his mind. The first impact of horror comes early with the burning of the wax models, whose melting features and limbs take on the repulsive aspect of decaying flesh, made worse by the two-colour process in which the film was made. Using another's hands to model for him, Igor sets up a new museum, killing and body-snatching to obtain corpses for special models which are coated with molten wax and put on exhibition. Finally, as he attacks Fay Wray, comes the terrible unmasking as his own wax mask cracks under her blow to reveal the hideous green scarred face beneath. Even Miss Wray admitted that, on the first take, she had been so shocked by the face behind the mask that she froze and was unable to continue!

To cash in on the short-lived revival of 3-D, Warner remade the film as *House of Wax* (1953), with Phyllis Kirk taking over the screaming from Fay Wray and Vincent Price, velvet-voiced and menacing in Gordon Bau's make-up as the crazed sculptor.

One of the most horrifying films of the genre was *Les Yeux Sans Visage* (*Eyes without a Face*), released in 1959. Directed by Georges Franju, the film is horrifying in its almost documentary approach to the story of Dr. Genessier (Pierre Brasseur), a mad surgeon who attempts to transplant the faces of kidnapped women on the disfigured face of his daughter, whose beauty he himself was responsible for destroying. Dr. Genessier shows the removal of the dead girls' features whole with an almost believable surgical accuracy that is nauseating. More horror is piled on as the daughter (Edith Scob) watches each new face decay, or as she wanders, a white mask of a face behind which only the eyes are living, through the cellars and rooms of the house, phoning her fiancé to hear his voice even though she is powerless to speak herself. In an appropriately Grand Guignol ending, the daughter stabs her father's assistant (Alida Valli) and lets loose savage dogs used by her father for experimental skin grafts. Not for the first time in screen horror, they tear their tormentor to shreds. Despite the melodrama of its plot, on which no less than six writers worked, the film delivers some genuinely haunting moments of fear in addition to its set pieces of absolute terror.

Spain's contribution to the 'masquerade' genre of horror films was *La Cara del Terror* in 1962. This was a monstrous melange of maniacs, mad scientists and masks, with mental patient Norma (Lisa Gaye) stowing away in the car of surgeon Dr. Taylor (Fernando Rey), and finally persuading him to try his new system of plastic surgery on her hideously disfigured face. He does the trick, restores her beauty, only to be attacked by her and left paralyzed while Norma, beautiful as long as she keeps applying Dr. Taylor's preservative, sets out on a trail of carnage and horror. While pushing an over-familiar hotel manager to his death down a lift shaft, she breaks the bottle of preserving fluid. Undaunted, she persuades her wealthy playboy suitor to marry her, but the honeymoon is ruined in a terrifying scene as the wind destroys her mask of a face. Not surprisingly, her husband flees from her in terror, only to have Norma run him down with the car! The climax comes when she returns to the partially recovered Dr. Taylor who has perfected his preserving fluid. In a fierce fight with the doctor's assistant, the now ugly and disfigured Norma is killed: the fluid spills from a table onto her dead face, and once more it returns to its plastic beauty!

Peter Cushing turned up in *Corruption* in 1967, a more surgical and nastier version of *Eyes Without a Face*, attempting to restore the face of his fiancée (Sue Lloyd), permanently disfigured when a flood lamp falls onto her face in a fight. With a combination of laser beams and pituitary glands snatched from corpses and dissected from murder victims, Cushing effects temporary, increasingly horrific 'cures' on Sue Lloyd. The film ends in an eruption of horror as the laser beam goes out of control, incinerating most of the cast! With its gratuitous images of physical unpleasantness, such as a severed head in a polythene bag kept in the refrigerator next to the dairy products, the film was an unworthy vehicle for Cushing's talents.

It was pleasant to see the ultimate in men behind the mask, Death himself, in the person of Cushing again, this time as Dr. Schreck, sinister mittened teller of tales to his fellow train-travellers in *Dr. Terror's House of Horrors* (1965) directed by Freddie Francis. As the travellers arrive at their destination, an eerie, steam-shrouded railway station in limbo, their fortune-telling companion Dr. Schreck turns, the mask of humanity fallen from him, to reveal beneath his hood the grinning skull of Death!

RIGHT *The 'Butcher of Baltimore', Patrick O'Neal, gets his hook into Laura Devon in the waxworks' film* Chamber of Horrors *(WB 1966).*

PRECEDING PAGES *Jekyll and Hyde 'Amicus style'. Christopher Lee as Marlowe/Blake in* I, Monster *(Amicus 1970).*

ABOVE *Rank Film Distributors' poster for* Hands of the Ripper *(Hammer 1971).*

ABOVE RIGHT *Vincent Price prepares to preserve Phyllis Kirk in the 3-D film* House of Wax *(WB 1953).*

RIGHT *The greatest screamer of them all, Fay Wray, awaits immersion in wax by the horribly scarred Lionel Atwill in Michael Curtiz's* Mystery of the Wax Museum *(WB 1933).*

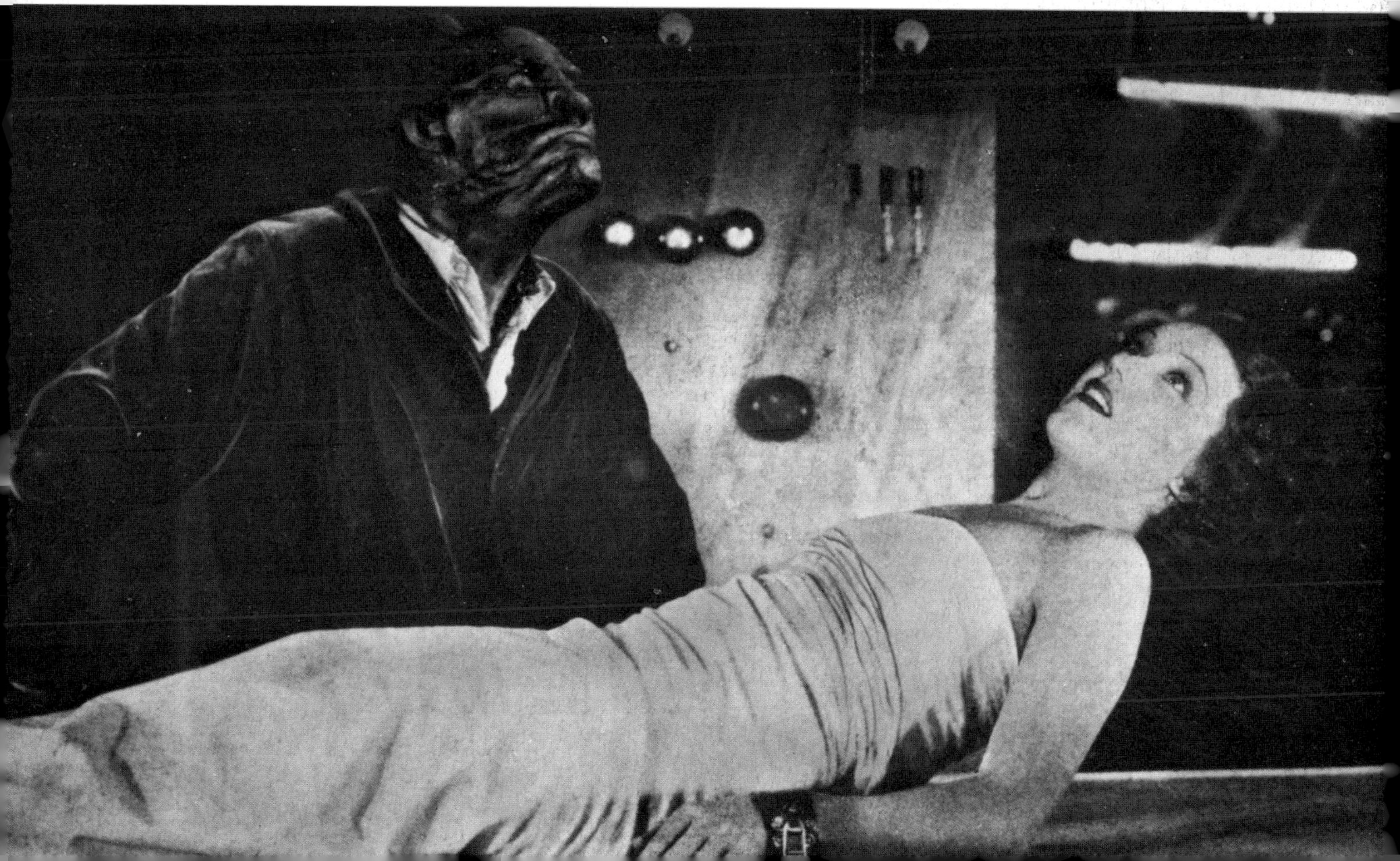

MEET THE LADIES!

"Here's to woman! Would that we could fall into her arms without falling into her hands!" Ambrose Bierce

ALTHOUGH FEWER in number than their male and monstrous counterparts, the ladies of screen horror are every bit as deadly, making up for their lack of numbers by the amount of sheer terror and all-round unpleasantness they have caused.

Women have formed part of the horror film from its earliest days, with a predilection towards metamorphosis into a veritable bestiary of monsters. The cat, in particular, has usually been to woman what the werewolf is to man. As early as 1910, audiences were thrilling to the French film version of the Aesop Fable *La Chatte Metamorphosée en Femme* (*The Cat That Was Changed into a Woman*), although the transformation is generally the other way around.

The Cat People (US 1942), one of the many 'highgrade, low budget' horror movies produced by Val Lewton for RKO Radio Pictures, is a masterpiece of the genre. *The Cat People* concerns Irena (Simone Simon) who, while born in Serbia, lives and works as a fashion designer in New York. As the result of certain events in her ancestors' past, she has the power to turn into a large and savage cat when her emotions become too strong. Because of her fear of intense emotion, she is unwilling to marry Kent Smith (Oliver Reed) but he eventually persuades her. She will not consummate their marriage, however, and Reed is driven by the lack of sex in their life to consult a psychiatrist and then to seek solace in the company of Alice (Jane Randolph). Irena becomes passionately jealous and as a result a huge, barely glimpsed cat makes several attempts on Alice's life. When the psychiatrist (Tom Conway) attempts to seduce Irena so as to purge her of her fears of sex and emotion, he is clawed to death as Irena becomes a savage beast once more. She is wounded in the struggle and makes her way to the city zoo where she dies by the cages of the great pacing cats which were her obsessive passion.

The film provided the horror cinema with one

LEFT *The lady strikes out. Anoushka Hempel attacks Christopher Mathews in Roy Ward Baker's* Scars of Dracula *(Hammer 1970).*
ABOVE *The ghostly brides of Bela Lugosi in* Dracula *(Universal 1931).*

ABOVE *Yutte Stensgaard proves that the female of the species is at least as deadly as the male in Jimmy Sangster's* Lust for a Vampire *(Hammer 1971).*
RIGHT *'Britain's First Lady of Horror', Barbara Steele, as the evil witch returning from death in* The Curse of the Crimson Altar *(Tigon British/AIP 1968).*

of its great female terrors in Simone Simon, whose strange, almost passive face and staccato movements hinted eerily at the dangerous beast below the surface. The three attacks of the cat beast are made genuinely terrifying by masterly use of shadow and sound. When the giant cat, always in shadow, pursues Alice through deserted streets by night, the terror of the scene builds up almost unendurably until, with the force almost of a physical blow, the sudden pneumatic hiss of a bus door announces Alice's rescue. Even greater in its horror impact is the next attack of the cat woman on the pathetically vulnerable Alice, this time trapped in the water of a deserted basement swimming pool. Around her shadows prowl the edges of the pool to merge and sway with the rippling light from the pool itself and the strange perspectives of the pool and surrounds. While Alice desperately treads water, Irena is seen in shadow, transformed into a huge cat, emitting magnified and distorted feral growls. At the return of Oliver the cat, never fully glimpsed but terrifyingly implied, disappears. Alice is saved, and the only tangible proof of her ordeal is her bathrobe at the edge of the pool, shredded by savage talons.

Finally, Alice and Oliver are trapped in a deserted drawing office, where they are stalked through the strange planes of light by the sound and shadow of the giant cat. Terror borders on the subliminal, the viewer 'seeing' images far worse than any shown on the screen. At the insistence of senior producers Lewton inserted one shot of an actual panther—the 'transformed' Irena—stalking the couple around the drawing office. For the rest, suggestion, editing, powerful use of light and sound culminate in scenes which make Irena an utterly horrifying screen monster.

Vincent Price starred in another horrifying film about a 'cat-woman'—*The Tomb of Ligeia* (1964). At the funeral of his wife Ligeia in 1821, Verden Fell (Vincent Price) dismisses the local priest's objection that Ligeia was not a Christian. Price counters that his wife will not rest 'because she is not dead', adding for good measure her philosophy, 'Man need not kneel before the angels nor lie in death forever but for the weakness of his feeble will'. Suddenly a black cat screeches and for an instant, in the coffin, Ligeia's eyes flick open. Price is stunned but triumphant, explaining it as a post-mortem muscular contraction. Ligeia is far from dead as both Fell and Lady Rowena Trevanion (Elizabeth Shepherd) are to find out! Lady Rowena, out hunting, rides away from the hunt to stare at the tombstone of Ligeia. Suddenly a

black cat hisses, the horse rears and Rowena is thrown, fainting as Fell appears. Fell carries her back to his vast Gothic Abbey home, where Rowena's father appears after the hunt with the body of a fox, which Fell tells them was once Ligeia's pet. As they talk, the fox's corpse disappears, but Fell explains that the cat has taken it.

Finding herself attracted to the strange Fell with his pale manner and bizarre dark glasses, Rowena jilts her companion Christopher (John Westbrook). But when she tries to kiss Fell, a cat flies between them, clawing Rowena's face. Fell agrees to have the cat killed, but later it steals his dark glasses and, gripping them daintily in her sharp teeth, in a scene of powerful horror, lures Rowena in pursuit up the crumbling heights of a perilous bell tower from which Rowena nearly falls to her death.

Despite these omens, Rowena weds Fell, only to have him abandon her after their honeymoon, to wander the ghostly abbey. Rowena, meanwhile, is terrified by a series of strange episodes where saucers of milk and dead foxes appear and disappear and where her dreams turn to stark terror when her embrace with Fell changes to her kissing Ligeia, and smothering in her black tresses. Her possession by Ligeia becomes more pronounced when, after Fell hypnotizes her, Rowena speaks with Ligeia's voice. Christopher, meanwhile, has Ligeia's coffin dug up, only to find the corpse gone and a wax effigy in its place.

The film reaches a climax of terror as Rowena turns into a feline form of Ligeia and Fell, a man possessed, attacks the black cat in a frenzy. After Ligeia is thrown into an altar of flames, the cat takes yet another form, blinding Fell as he grapples with Ligeia until they are both destroyed as the abbey is consumed by fire. Dead at last, the cat-Ligeia leaves Rowena, who is carried back to safety by Christopher.

After the cat comes the snake. No doubt in a belated attempt to make good the damage done in The Garden of Eden, women have been changing into snakes from the beginning of the cinema. In 1912, audiences at *The Reincarnation of Karma* were horrified to see Rosemary Thebe, playing an Indian dancing girl, turn into a ten-foot serpent after being cursed by the High Priest of the Temple of Innocent Manhood. She was a patient woman, however, waiting two thousand years to wreak her vengeance on the reincarnation of the High Priest! Britain's first horror film also featured an Indian girl who was seen to change into a snake and sink her fangs into the hunter who had shot her. Curiously, the film was entitled *The Vampire* (GB 1913) but with women, horror, like beauty, is also only skin deep and capable of infinite meanings. Two years later came *Heba The Snake Woman* who repeated the horrific pattern set by the lady in *The Vampire*, except that as an Aztec she presumably changed into a poisonous South American snake.

Forty years passed before Faith Domergue carried on the tradition in *Cult of the Cobra* (US 1955). She was the strangely sibilant Lisa Moya, High Priestess of an Eastern sect of snake-worshippers who emigrated to America where, endowed with the ability to become a snake, she proceeded to despatch all the ex-servicemen rash enough to photograph her forbidden rites!

Susan Travis was Atheris, *The Snake Woman* (GB 1960), the unfortunate child of a mother injected during pregnancy with snake venom as a cure for insanity. Escaping the burning of her father's laboratory by the ever-available villagers, the cold-blooded child with no eye-lids grew to womanhood among a population decimated by snake-bite and amidst rumours of a strange snake-woman seen wandering the North Country moors. Finally, responding to the strains of a handy snake-charmer's flute played by Prentice of Scotland Yard, the beautiful Atheris changed into a cobra and was killed by the resourceful policeman, only to change back into the corpse of Atheris.

Hammer, using the Cornish sets already employed in *The Plague of The Zombies*, offered Jacqueline Pearce, in chilling make-up by Roy Ashton, as *The Reptile* (GB 1960). As Ann Franklyn, victim of an obscure Malayan sect, she lived by the bubbling sulphur springs in her father's cellar. Emerging from her hibernation she shed her snake skin for the new season's model and sank her fangs into the film's hero and Mad Peter among others, the final victim being her own father. She later perished in the obligatory holocaust. She was a true monster of horror, described by the publicists as having: 'Bared teeth dripping deadly venom; forked tongue flashing awful intent; blood-red eyes holding grim, hypnotic sway; repellent scales; lizard-like paws. . . . This is The Reptile, poised to strike . . . !

Universal had the idea of giving additional proof to Darwin's Theory of Evolution with *Captive Wild Woman* (US 1943) in which the improbably named Aquanetta was transformed from orang-utang to woman by John Carradine. Sadly, the resultant horror, Paula Dupree, reverted to ape under stress, particularly when her sexual passions were aroused, and was finally shot. Too good a monster to die so soon, she was revived the follow-

RIGHT *Jacqueline Pearce turns into a snake-woman in* The Reptile *(Hammer 1966).*
BELOW *Vincent Price bandages the foot of the possessed Elizabeth Shepherd in Roger Corman's film of female evil,* The Tomb of Ligeia *(Anglo-Amalgamated/AIP 1964).*

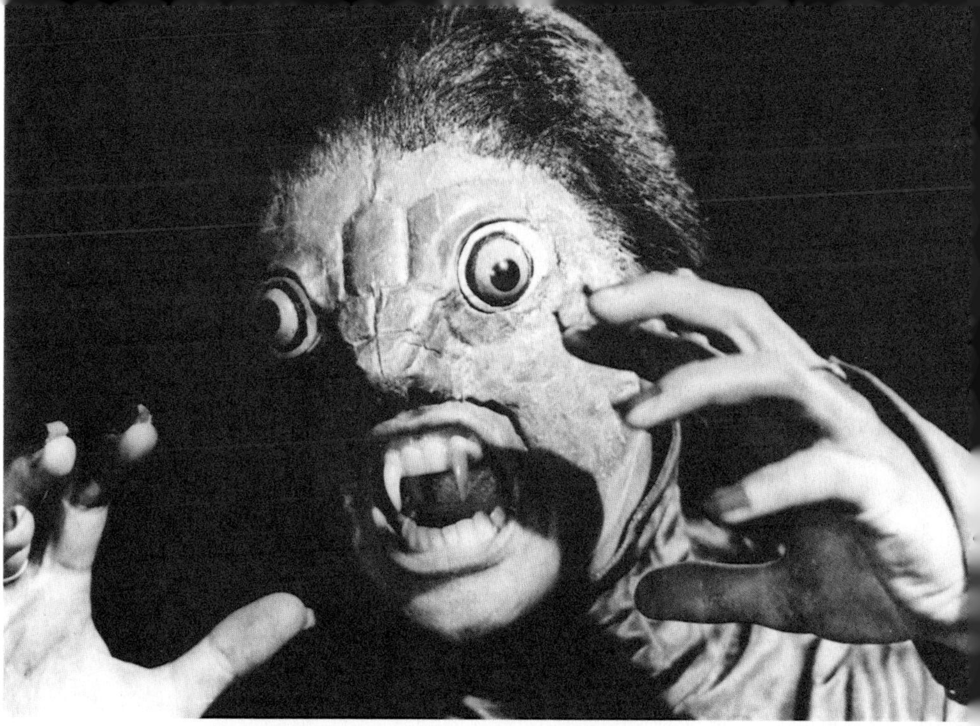

ing year, again as Paula Dupree, by Dr. Fletcher (J. Carrol Naish) in *Jungle Woman* (US 1944). Once more she perished as an ape, and although she returned once more in *Jungle Captive* (US 1945), this time Paula Dupree was played by Vicky Lane, Aquanetta having decided that twice was enough for any ape-woman. Vicky Lane too was shot, this time as she attempted to save another girl from the surgery that was to remove her brain and transplant it into Paula's. The character remained dead as did the series.

Most of the horrific ladies have been the wives, children or other relatives of their more famous monstrous counterparts. *Dracula's Daughter* (US 1936) followed on the success of Lugosi's Dracula with pallid faced Gloria Holden as the titled Countess Marya Zaleska. She proved a suitably horrific bearer of the Dracula name, notching up a good number of victims in a film subtly hinting at the lesbian aspects of vampirism in the scenes with her female victims. Van Helsing, fresh from his triumphs in despatching Lugosi, was the first to pronounce ringingly: 'We must find it and destroy it!' as Gloria Holden once more put Transylvania under the vampire's thrall. He was on hand to utter her epitaph as, staked through the heart with a wooden arrow, she perished. 'She was beautiful when she died—a hundred years ago!'

Gloria Talbott played Janet, *Daughter of Dr. Jekyll* (US 1957) in a film replete with werewolf killings for which she was blamed until proved innocent, and her guardian—the true inheritor of the nasty and hitherto unknown secrets of the late Dr. Jekyll—had been despatched with a stake through his heart by the alert villagers! *Frankenstein's Daughter* (US 1958) emerged twenty three years after Elsa Lanchester's horrific *Bride of Frankenstein*, but the daughter, played by Sandra Knight, was by comparison only a pallid slice of the old cadaver. The unwitting victim of the experiments of young Oliver Frank (enstein), she wanders the city as a nocturnal monster before the evil Oliver, his second monster, and the grotesque halfwit gardener who has been helping him, are destroyed in a fire which consumes the laboratory from which Oliver has been operating. Finally the Baron's daughter managed to have yet another fling when, in *Jesse James Meets Frankenstein's Daughter* (1965), she managed to change a wounded outlaw into yet another monster!

Hammer added another 'classic' monster with Terence Fisher's *The Gorgon* (GB 1964). Filled with chilling menace, the film was set in the Transylvanian village of Vandorf, terrorized by a series of killings in which the victims have turned to stone. The Gorgon Megaera is found in the ruins of the nearby Castle Borski, but the discoverer sees her, and is himself turned to stone, having just time to summon help in the form of his son Paul and Paul's tutor, Professor Meinster (Christopher Lee in a fine set of whiskers and playing, for once, the avenger!). Eventually the Gorgon is found to be in possession of the beautiful Carla Hoffman (Barbara Shelley), assistant and ex-patient of the sinister Namaroff (Peter Cushing). Meinster finally kills Namaroff and beheads Megaera. As the spirit of the Gorgon leaves the body, the head turns back into the lovely dead features of Carla. Roy Ashton's make-up for the Gorgon, haloed with a hissing, striking frieze of serpents made Megaera a true and unique female monster.

Hammer too, were responsible for the creation of *Countess Dracula* (GB 1970), which, despite its title, dealt with blood and murder, corruption and decay instead of vampirism. Ingrid Pitt, playing the ageing Countess Elisabeth Nasady, discovers the gruesome secret of rejuvenation which can only be accomplished by bathing in the blood of young girls. Restored to youth and beauty, she arranges the abduction of her daughter Ilona, and, posing as the girl, seduces and becomes engaged to Imre Toth. She finds her new youthfulness short-lived however, and another girl is killed for her blood. The next victim's blood does not work the miracle and she learns that only the blood of virgins will preserve her 'youth'. Despite watching Elisabeth bathing in blood, Imre, repelled yet attracted, agrees to go on with their wedding. But as she speaks the marriage vows, Elisabeth suddenly and appallingly crumbles into hag-like old age, killing Imre as she strikes out at her own daughter in one last desperate attempt to get the blood she needs. Ingrid Pitt conveys in a film replete with horror, the decay and corruption constantly lurking below the surface of the beautiful 'young' Countess, making her physically attractive even when she is at her most evil, with blood streaming over her breasts and body.

Certainly one of the youngest and arguably the most shocking of all horror monsters is Jane (Chloe

Two scenes from The Gorgon *(Hammer 1964). Richard Pasco prowls the Transylvanian castle* (top right) *in search of the monster, and* (right) *later comes across the body of one of the Gorgon's victims turned to stone.*
FAR RIGHT *Driven to madness by the effects of the 'evil' serum, Lorna Heilbron flees the house in* The Creeping Flesh *(Tigon British/World Film Services 1972).*

Fatal Females!
ABOVE FAR LEFT *Tallulah Bankhead in her last film role as the demented Mrs. Trefoile in* Fanatic *(Hammer-Seven Arts 1965).*
ABOVE LEFT *Janette Scott threatens Fenella Fielding in the colour remake of* The Old Dark House *(Hammer-William Castle 1966).*
LEFT *Glynis Johns takes a hammer to her husband prior to bottling him in pieces in* Vault of Horror *(Metromedia/Amicus 1973).*
ABOVE *Chloe Franks brings terror to Christopher Lee as the most chilling of all female monsters in Peter Duffell's* The House that Dripped Blood *(Amicus 1970).*
RIGHT *Judith Lang becomes a vampire in* Count Yorga, Vampire *(Erica/AIP 1970).*

Franks) in Peter Duffell's *The House That Dripped Blood* (GB 1970). In the episode *Sweets to the Sweet*, she plays the daughter of widower John Reid (Christopher Lee) who engages Ann Norton (Nyree Dawn Porter) as Governess to the child. Ann finds Jane absolutely angelic, an aura of soft blonde hair framing a face of innocence and beauty. She is appalled to find the child forbidden to play with toys or other children, and to have a terror for fire. Charmed by Jane, Ann coaxes her into the enchantment of fire and buys her a doll. Her father, throwing the doll on the fire, is tormented by agonizing pains. Even when he explains to Ann that Jane, like her mother, is a witch and bent on killing him, Ann refuses to believe it until she finds Jane with a wax doll cradled in her arms, sticking pins into it. In a finale of carefully mounted and powerful horror, Ann begs the child to give her the doll. Instead, Jane turns and throws it on the fire. As the camera closes in on the obscene image of the melting figure, the horror explodes into a chilling off-screen scream of animal agony as John Reid dies. Duffell manages to suggest both the surface charm and angelic presence of Jane, particularly in idyllic scenes as she and her Governess walk through soft green exteriors, and the evil of the child's cold-blooded murder of her father.

Ending our tribute to the fairer but certainly not weaker sex, at one extreme there is the eight-inch high *Devil Doll* (US 1936) who, under the influence of the malevolent thought-control of Lionel Barrymore, changes from a child's toy, cradled in the arms of a sleeping girl, into a killer, climbing along the bars of the cot like some deadly zoo creature and down to the floor, finally to scale the bedclothes of her sleeping victim. There she moves along the body of the snoring banker, suddenly to plunge a poisoned stiletto into his arm. At the other extreme, the ultimate award for monstrous womanhood should go to Dorothy Provine who, as *The 30-Foot Bride of Candy Rock*, gave some of his own medicine to Lou Costello, one half of the movie team that seems at one time or another to have engaged all the great monsters of the cinema!

BELOW *The eternal fall-guy, Elisha Cook Jnr., gets the treatment from black vampire Ketty Lestér in* Blacula *(AIP 1972).*
RIGHT *Another lady vampire takes a stake between the ribs—Valerie van Ost in* The Satanic Rites of Dracula *(Hammer 1973).*

MADMEN, DEMENTED DOCTORS AND PSYCHOPATH SCIENTISTS

"Science is always wrong: it never solves a problem without creating ten more." George Bernard Shaw

A GENERAL distrust and fear of doctors and scientists sustains the steady flow of mad-doctor, screwball-scientist and maniac-next-door films which have kept Messrs Chaney Senior and Junior, Karloff, Lugosi, Cushing, Price and Lee fully occupied in the front rank of screen horror, ably supported by such lunatic stalwarts as Peter Lorre, Lionel Atwill, John Carradine and George Zucco. Whether they are born mad, achieve madness or have madness thrust upon them, they seldom bemoan their fate, exulting like Dr. Praetorius in *The Bride of Frankenstein*: 'Alone you have created a man. Now together we will create his mate!' or ruefully confiding, as Jack Griffin, The Invisible Man, felt: 'I meddled in things that man must leave alone!' Fortunately for us and the horror film, nobody has ever seemed likely to take Mr. Griffin's warning to heart.

From his first major screen incarnation in 1931, the screen's prototype evil genius was Baron Frankenstein. But he had his rivals, among them the club-footed *Dr. X* (1932). This role was the horror film debut of dapper British mad-doctor stalwart, Lionel Atwill, although here the club-footed medic turned out to be a sinister red herring for the vile moon-murderer, one-armed Preston Foster. Foster, who chilled the blood by his repellent habit of tearing the left deltoid muscle from his victims' backs and devouring it, made up for

LEFT *Karloff at his most sinister as Mord, the club-footed executioner in* Tower of London *(Universal 1939).*
ABOVE *Make them laugh! Kenneth Williams, Fenella Fielding and Tom Clegg in Gerald Thomas'* Carry on Screaming *(Anglo-Amalgamated 1966).*

his lack of a second arm by synthesizing a 'spare' as required from the artificial flesh he had discovered. Fay Wray supplied the perfect menaced heroine, and director Michael Curtiz deftly paced the horror in the standard old dark house, emphasizing it with the snappy Thirties humour of some of the dialogue.

Paramount contributed a minor, often tasteless but ultimately terrifying film in Erle C. Kenton's *The Island of Lost Souls* (US 1932) (GB Title: *The Island of Doctor Moreau*). Charles Laughton gave a bravura performance as the grotesque and sadistic Doctor Moreau, banished from civilized society because of his vile attempts at cross breeding, who strives in his 'House of Pain' to turn animals into men. A hirsute Bela Lugosi played the Sayer of The Law, led by Moreau, whip in hand, as the monstrosities—dogmen, pigmen and others too far past bestiality or humanity to recognize—chanted their Creed: 'What is the Law? Not to spill blood, not to chase other men, not to go on all fours, not to eat flesh: That is the Law. Are we not men?' Finally, in an attack by Lugosi, Moreau is destroyed by his deformed creations in his own 'House of Pain'.

Karloff and Lugosi, the reigning kings of horror, met in Universal's *The Black Cat* (US 1934). The two main characters shared equal billing and equal screen time, although it was Karloff who was the maniac and Lugosi on the side of Good, playing Dr. Vitus Verdegast with his usual aura of menace. Karloff was the crazed Hjalmar Poelzig, carrying out Devil worship in the futuristic glass and concrete palace he had built on the site of his old fortress. Director Edgar G. Ulmer, one-time set designer with Murnau, eschewed the traditional flights of stairs and cobwebbed dungeons for strange, stark modernism which helped underline Karloff's dominating and evil performance. The two finally confront each other when Lugosi saves Karloff's intended human sacrifice of an American girl at a Black Mass. Karloff is tied up and skinned alive; Lugosi, as a last gesture to tidy up loose plot ends, blows up the castle and with it the corpse of Karloff's murdered wife which had been kept on view under glass! The film provided a superb vehicle for the two stars, with lashings of horror, sadism, Black Magic and necrophilia to delight the most discriminating palate! (The British Censor stepped in once again, removed all traces of Satanism and let the film out emasculated as *The House of Doom*.)

Peter Lorre, the chilling child-killer of Fritz Lang's *M*, made his American debut in a re-make of *The Hands of Orlac*, entitled *Mad Love* (US 1935). Lorre was Doctor Gogol, surgical genius and madman, happily grafting a murderer's hands onto the wrists of Orlac (Colin Clive), a concert pianist who had lost his hands in a train smash. Orlac becomes insane with fear when he finds that his new hands come from the guillotined knife-thrower (Edward Brophy) but, in a tremendous climax as a totally mad Gogol pursues Orlac's wife (Frances Drake), the knife-throwing talents so obligingly supplied by the mad surgeon enable Orlac to foil him.

The Lady and the Monster, the first of several versions of Curt Siodmak's novel, *Donovan's Brain*, featured Erich von Stroheim, teutonically insane, as the doctor who removes the undamaged brain from the dead financier W. H. Donovan, to keep it alive in a tank of fluid where it soon starts to influence others' wills, thus obtaining surrogate bodies.

Val Lewton, king of the RKO second-feature horrors, made a fine film of fright *The Body Snatcher* with Henry Daniell as Doctor Knox of Edinburgh, purchasing corpses snatched by Karloff and his assistant Lugosi. Based on Robert Louis Stevenson's version of the Burke and Hare story, Robert Wise directed it with a fine flair for the frightening moments. There is real evil in Karloff and Lugosi's body-snatching of young girls from dark alleys and the climax ranks as one of the most terrifying in the history of screen horror, with the demented Doctor Knox driving a hearse hell for leather with Karloff's corpse falling out of its shroud beside him, while the dead man's voice echoes in his mind, 'Never get rid of me, never get rid of me,' counterpointing the panicked galloping of the horses.

The Fly (US 1958) marked two firsts: the more prosaic was that the film was the first horror movie to be made in Cinemascope. The second was a landmark, with Vincent Price, velvet-voiced as ever, appearing in his first horror picture. He was on the side of good this time, however, as the brother of the dead André Delambre (Al Hedison), trying to save André's wife from madness and piecing together from her the hideous story of her husband's death. Kurt Neumann directed James Clavell's script for all it was worth, producing a colour masterpiece of terror and repulsion. Scene after scene piles horror more thickly, nearly always managing to avoid slipping from the terrifying to

RIGHT *Ursula Howells as the female werewolf in Freddie Francis'* Dr. Terror's House of Horrors *(Amicus 1964).*

Nazis on ice! Philip Gilbert takes inventory of The Frozen Dead *(Goldstar 1966), preserved for the future.*

the risible. Scientist André Delambre constructs a 'matter transmitter' which works perfectly on inanimate objects, disintegrating them into their constituent atoms and sending them to be reassembled in the receiver at the other end of his basement laboratory. The first animal experiment fails with the family's pet cat ending as 'a stream of cat atoms' accompanied by a despondent mewing!

The bloody grotesqueries begin when André attempts to transmit himself: he fails to see the fly in the transmitter with him, and arrives in the receiver with the fly's head and arm. The scene as he paces the laboratory, with his head and arm covered by a black cloth, and the revolting animal noises as he 'eats' culminate in his wife (Patricia Owens) seeing the insane monster her husband has become. She stares screaming at the grotesque insect head with its multi-faceted eyes, while a subjective shot shows hundreds of tiny screaming heads in a mosaic of terror covering the cinemascope screen. Horror mounts as André wrestles with a mind rapidly going insane, while he tries to direct wife, son and brother in a search for the fly with his head. As his madness mounts, he finds himself unable to control his fly's claw, and in a scene that must have inspired Peter Sellers' Dr. Strangelove his human hand wrestles for supremacy with the huge insect arm that has begun to possess volition of its own. The climax is gruesome and logical as André persuades his wife to destroy all traces of the insane creature he has become, killing him by crushing the insect head and arm to pulp in a hydraulic press. Neumann forces the audience to share her horror and revulsion when she has to repeat the pulping operation after the fly's arm has escaped the first smash of the press. The culminating nastiness occurs when the fly with André's head is trapped in a web and—screaming for help in a tiny voice saturated with terror—is eaten by a spider. The scene just manages to come off, despite the fact that horrified onlookers Price and Herbert Marshall had great difficulty in maintaining straight faces during the many takes needed to get their reactions.

Needless to say, there were sequels, with André's son Philippe (Brett Halsey) suffering the same fate as his father when he carried on transmitting in *The Return of The Fly* (US 1959), with a kindly Vincent Price on hand again to survey the horror. Don Sharp directed the third of the series in Britain, with father Henri Delambre (Brian Donlevy) and son Martin (George Baker) still working on the same lines but with even more horrible results in *The Curse of The Fly* (GB 1965). This time they produce not flies but semi-human monsters, Martin's first wife, and two laboratory assistants, all victims of the curse of the experimenting Delambres. Stan Simmons achieves a dubious niche in screen horror history by playing the singular result of two monsters joined in a transmission to London! Vincent Price is sadly missed, but the film is not without its moments, notably the half-glimpsed monsters held captive in the stables.

Another doctor driven mad by the grotesque results of his experiments was Ray Milland as Dr. Xavier in Roger Corman's *X—The Man With X-Ray Eyes* (US 1963). The ending is a classic moment of screen horror as Milland, crazed by the vision of his X-ray eyes—the result of an unproven serum—wanders into the tent of an itinerant preacher. His eyes are black holes against the colour of his face. The preacher continues with his sermon: '. . . if thine eye offend thee, pluck it out.' Milland raises his hands over his tortured eyes and brings them down again. The screen freezes on a chilling close-up: The black pits have vanished—only bloody red holes remain where once were Xavier's eyes!

Vincent Price turns up as a full-blooded mad scientist in *Scream and Scream Again* (GB 1969), carrying out sophisticated surgical procedures to produce a new race of super-human composite beings before he is killed by inscrutable Christopher Lee, a civil servant who turns out not to be so civil after all. As always, Price delivers his lines with relish and one almost sympathizes with him as he dunks an over-inquisitive snooper in a bath of acid. As urbane and mysterious as ever, Vincent Price is seen again in *The Oblong Box* (GB 1969), keeping his disfigured brother Edward chained up in his 19th-century mansion. When Edward attempts to escape by feigning death, he ends up buried alive. Scaring both the audience and the surgeon about to perform an autopsy on him, Edward gets off the dissecting slab and, masked in red, embarks on an orgy of revenge and destruction. Unable to free himself from the curse that has driven him insane, he returns to his brother's mansion, where he learns that the curse was meant for Price and not him. Price then shoots Edward who, before he dies manages to bite him savagely on the hand. Later, as Price's wife comes to call him for dinner, she sees him becoming horribly disfigured.

LEFT *Ingrid Pitt with victim surveys the ravages of advancing corruption in* Countess Dracula *(Hammer 1971).*

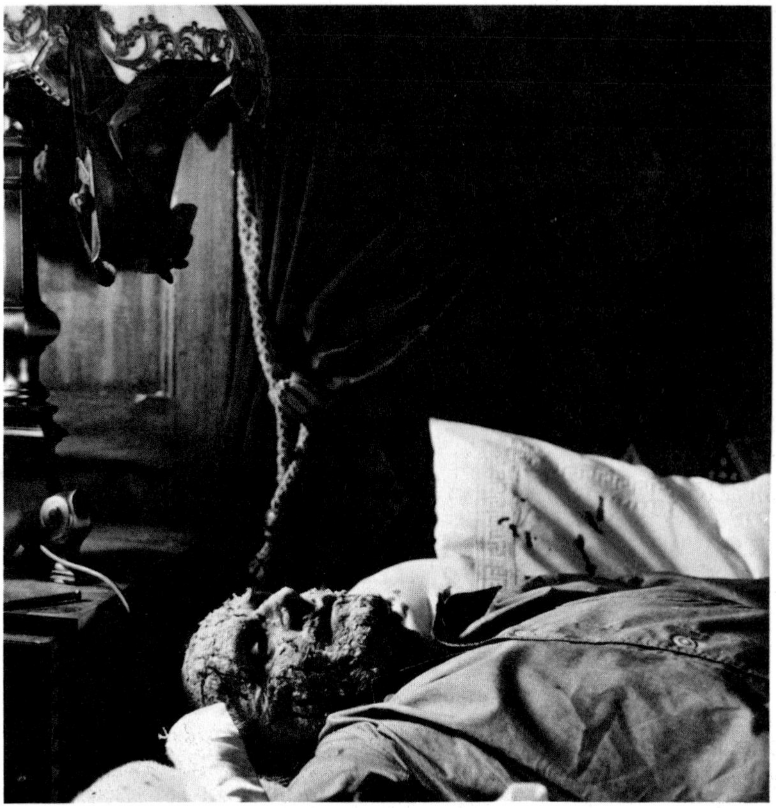

LEFT *Edward Burnham falls victim to one of the 'Biblical plagues' wreaked by Vincent Price as* The Abominable Dr. Phibes *(AIP 1971).*
RIGHT *Peter Lorre as Dr. Gogol, the mad surgeon in MGM's 1935 version of 'The Hands of Orlac'*—Mad Love.
FAR RIGHT *The unfortunate result of botched matter-transmission from* The Curse of the Fly *(20th Century-Fox/Lippert 1965).*
BELOW *Patrick O'Hara* (left) *as half guineapig/half man and total failure of an experiment by Brett Halsey in* The Return of the Fly *(20th Century-Fox 1959), and Vincent Price* (right) *battles with the title monster in the same film.*

In *The Abominable Dr. Phibes* (GB 1971) Price was back again wreaking vengeance on the members of the surgical team who years before had failed to save his wife on the operating table. The horribly disfigured Phibes, scarred for life as the result of a car crash, is given to musical bouts on the giant electric pipe organ that is the centrepiece of his lavishly decorated home. He suffers the double handicap of having to speak through an electronic voice pipe plugged into the side of his neck and of having to eat through a similar orifice! Assisted by his beautiful helper Vulnavia (Virginia North), Phibes despatches his victims by restaging the ten curses visited upon Pharaoh. One victim is stung to death by bees in a re-enactment of the plague of boils, another killed by bats, a third covered with a green fluid whipped up with chef-like gusto by Price, making her irresistible to the locusts which Phibes then looses to devour her! Inspector Trout (Peter Jeffrey), unable to prevent the killings, has trouble detaching the unfortunate Dr. Whitcombe from the wall to which he is pinned by a unicorn. Trout can only mutter that the horn must 'Have a lefthand thread!' Finally it is the turn of the leader of the surgeons, Dr. Vesalius, who has been helping the police, to have the curse of the death of the first-born visited upon him. In best mad-scientist tradition Phibes phones to tell him that his son is on an operating table below a phial of acid which is about to fall on him. Vesalius (Joseph Cotten) has only six minutes to operate and remove the key locking the operating table in place before the acid drops. He manages to release the boy, but not before Phibes has sealed himself away with his wife's preserved corpse!

Colour, set design, playing and Robert Fuest's direction make this one of the Seventies' most enjoyable and at the same time, horrifying horror films. The ten curses of Phibes give rise to some genuinely bizarre terrors and the major criticism is the waste through his electronic neck trumpet of Price's superb voice. In the sequel, *Dr. Phibes Rises Again*, rejuvenated by fresh blood replacing the embalming fluid in his veins, Phibes follows antiquarian Biederbeck to Egypt to seek the elixir of life with which to revivify his wife. These two films firmly establish Price as the perfect screen madman for the Sixties and Seventies.

More than any other film maker, Roger Corman succeeded in making a special genre of horror with his skilful movies based on the stories of Edgar Allen Poe. Made in the Sixties, these films, despite absurdly small budgets and a need to appeal to teenage audiences, established Corman as a serious director, far removed from the earlier B-feature quickies. The series incorporated impressive set designs by Daniel Haller, while Floyd Crosby's lush use of colour, and, above all, the acting of Vincent Price, Boris Karloff, Peter Lorre and Basil Rathbone, gave atmospheric distinction to the

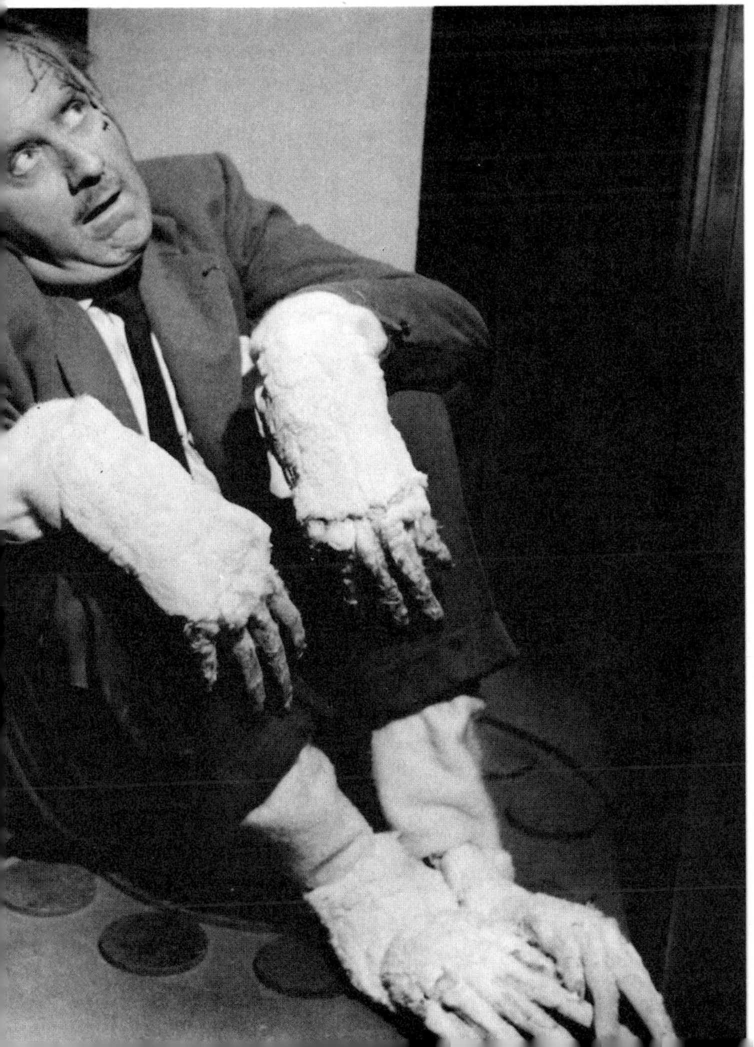

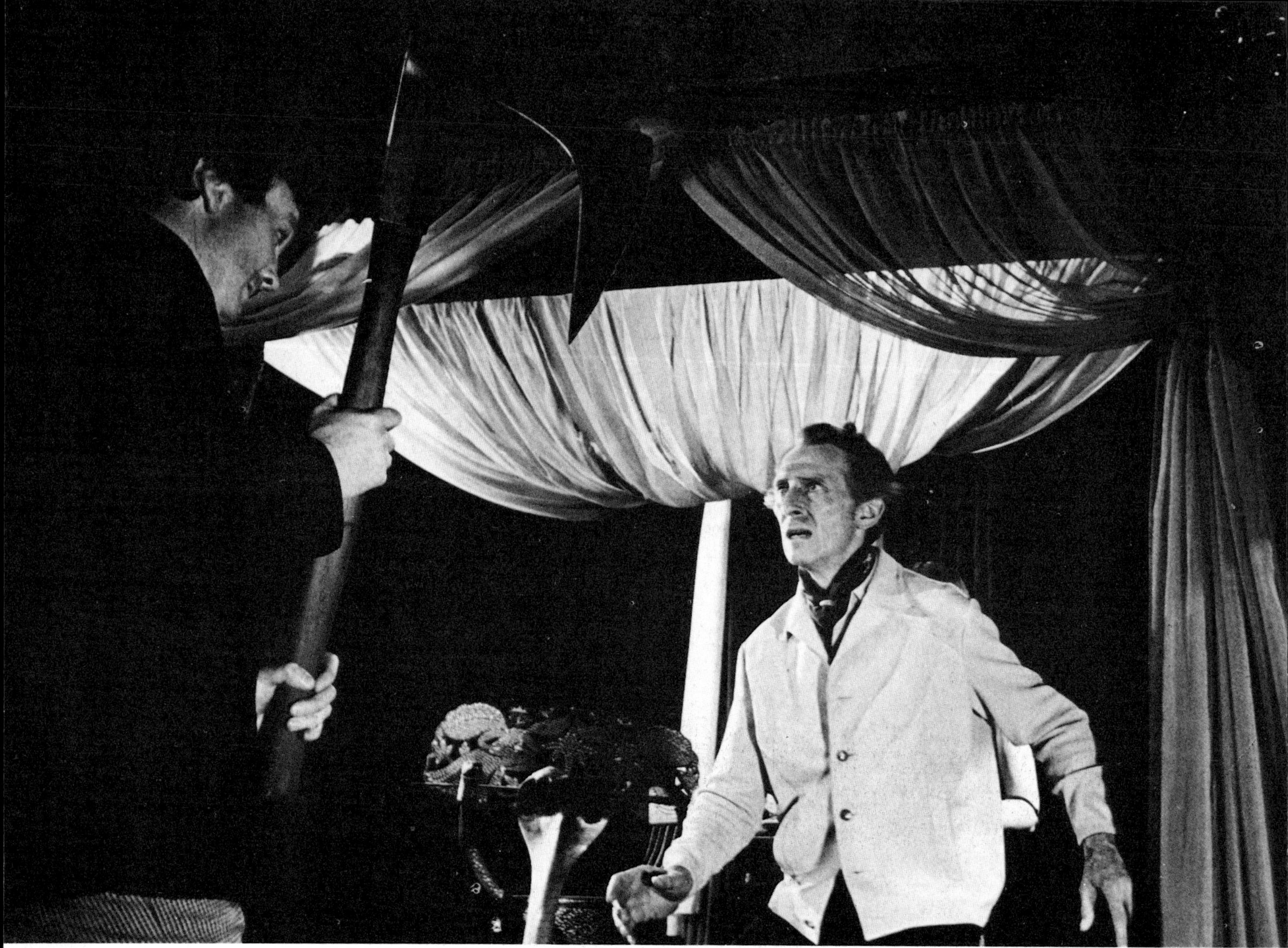

films.

The Fall of the House of Usher (US 1960) began the satisfying relationship between Corman, Price and Poe. The film begins promisingly with Philip Winthrop (Mark Damon) riding to the House of Usher to see his fiancée Madeline (Myrna Fahey), through a nightmare landscape of wreathed mists and stark trees. From the first entrance of Roderick Usher (Vincent Price), albino-haired and pale, suffering agonies at the smallest sound, the slightest abrasion on his skin, Corman relentlessly winds up the spring of terror.

When Philip refuses to leave without Madeline, Roderick Usher explains that, like him, she carries the taint of the Ushers, a strange madness which Roderick is determined shall die with them. Stubbornly Philip remains, attempting to get Madeline to leave with him. Attempts upon his life have the effect of making him more determined to remain, but already the curse of the Ushers is taking effect. In a terrifying visit to the family crypt, Madeline faints when a coffin inexplicably crashes at their feet. Later Philip finds her fully dressed in the room to which she has been carried, apparently dead. Roderick Usher has placed her in her coffin in the chapel insisting upon immediate burial.

The following morning Philip learns from the butler, Bristol, that his fiancée had been subject to cataleptic fits. He faces Roderick with the ghastly fact that he has buried his sister alive. Roderick, with the calm obsession of insanity, agrees, but tells him that it was done out of love and that Madeline is finally dead, and with her the taint that has haunted the Usher family.

Horror comes that night when, unable to sleep, Philip seeks Madeline's coffin, only to find the lid open, clawed and bloodied on the inside, and a trail of bloodstains leading to a hidden door. Possessed of superhuman strength and totally insane from her experiences, Madeline attacks Philip and, when he breaks away from her, seeks and attacks the man who buried her alive.

As a storm breaks and the House of Usher begins to fall, Philip watches impotently as sister and brother struggle in a mad embrace until the ceiling crashes down upon them. The butler drags Philip away from the house and then returns to perish in the inferno that destroys the House of Usher.

The Pit and The Pendulum (US 1961) consolidated Corman as interpreter of Poe. Once again Richard Matheson contributed a literate and never anachronistic script fron Poe's story, and Price seized the opportunities the role of Nicholas Medina provided. Daniel Haller came up with more superb

ABOVE LEFT *Peter Cushing battles with Wolfe Morris in* The House That Dripped Blood *(Amicus 1970).*
BELOW LEFT *Vincent Price as Count Prospero with Jane Asher in* The Masque of The Red Death *(Alta Vista/Anglo Amalgamated 1964).*
ABOVE *Vincent Price in Roger Corman's* The Pit and the Pendulum *(AIP 1961).*
BELOW *Raised from the dead, Vincent Price liquefies over evil mesmerist Basil Rathbone in Roger Corman's* Tales of Terror *(AIP 1962).*

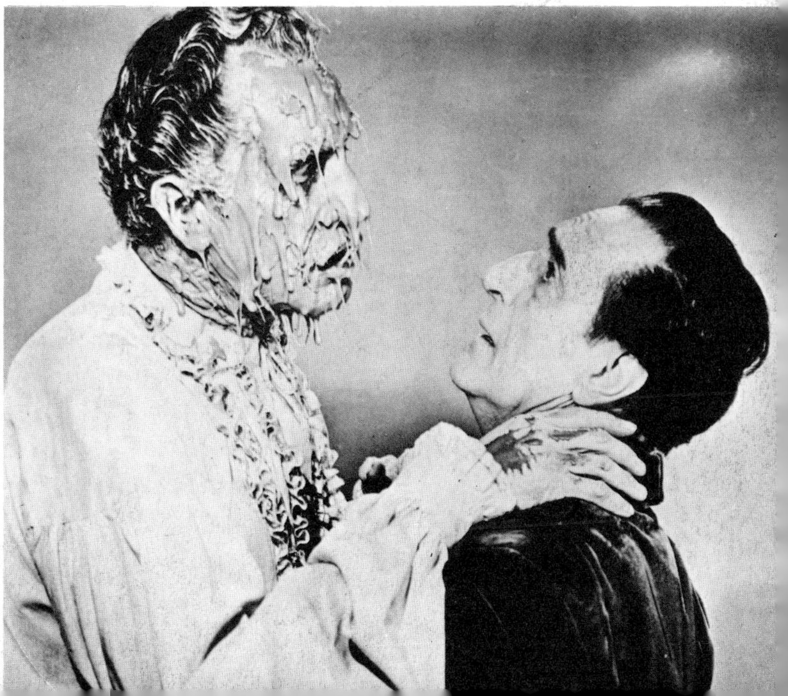

sets, particularly the torture chamber and the pendulum of the title, and Floyd Crosby once more photographed in suitably lurid colour. John Kerr is more than adequate in the juvenile lead, while Barbara Steele adds her own brand of strange facial horror. The film ends with Price pushed to his death in the pit and Miss Steele, unable to summon help, is left locked in a steel box in the torture chamber, to starve to death.

The sequence of the pendulum itself, swishing and slicing its way lower and lower towards the prostrate body of John Kerr is pure screen horror, made all the more potent by the incisive use of sound and by the awful inevitability of the mechanism. The British distributors of *The Pit and The Pendulum* offered '£10,000 If You Die of Fright!' going on to explain that the first person to die from fear while watching the film was automatically insured for that sum! They were lucky not to have had to pay out—although the film was again short—89 minutes—the tension never let up until the final dénouement, with the film ending on a close-up of Barbara Steele's eyes filled with terror gazing out into space through the bars of what was to be her coffin.

Tales of Terror (US 1962) was a compendium of three Poe stories again adapted by Richard Matheson, designed by Daniel Haller and photographed by Floyd Crosby. Price appeared in all three stories, in the first as the alcoholic Locke, in mourning for 26 years for his dead wife Morella whose death he blames on their only child Leonora (Maggie Pierce). When she returns, she is horrified to discover the mummified body of her mother, the face still contorted in a snarl of hatred against the daughter she blamed for her own untimely death. That night the spirit of Morella takes possession of Leonora and kills her. In his horror at finding that the mummy is now that of his daughter, Locke drops the candle he has been holding and the bedclothes and curtains catch fire, destroying Locke and the spirit of his wife as they struggle together. If this first story relied rather heavily upon Corman's predilection for stock shots of crashing waves and a final conflagration, it exercised considerable power to shock.

Price was joined by Lorre in the second of the three episodes, *The Black Cat*, in which Matheson also incorporated sections from Poe's *The Cask of Amontillado*, allowing Price and Lorre to indulge in a beautifully acted comedy scene of rip-roaring drunken boasting and wine tasting, before Lorre drugs Price and walls him up in the cellar with his unfaithful wife, Annabel. Later the police suspect the hallucinating Lorre and hearing the hideous wailing of a cat, they tear down the cellar wall to find the corpses of Price and Annabel. Perched on Annabel's head is Pluto, her pet black cat on whom she had lavished her affections after her husband's constant ill-treatment of her.

The final story, *The Facts In the Case of M. Valdemar* returned to Poe's obsession with catalepsy. Basil Rathbone played the totally unscrupulous mesmerist Carmichael, who uses his powers to ease the pain of the dying Valdemar (Vincent Price). Despite strong opposition from Valdemar's wife Helene and their doctor, Carmichael persuades Valdemar to allow himself to be hypnotized at the point of death, thus cheating the inevitable. For months Valdemar lies in a cataleptic trance, apparently dead yet able to communicate through closed lips. Eventually Carmichael attempts to get Valdemar to tell Helene to give up Doctor James and marry him, but when Helene yields, Valdemar awakes from his trance and, clasping Carmichael to him in a grip of slime, liquefies into a putrescent pool, with Carmichael dying of fright. This last sequence is terrifyingly presented and comes as an almost welcome climax to the eerie mood of tension and fear of the unknown built up by the acting, direction and by the weird soundtrack used in the trance scenes.

Corman's next Poe adaptation, *The Haunted Palace* (US 1963), was a combination of stories by Poe and H. P. Lovecraft, written for the screen this time by Charles Beaumont, and once more featuring the same technical team on the set design and cinematography. This time Price plays a dual role with relish, carefully defining the two characters of Joseph Curwen, burned to death as a witch in the New England village of Arkham in 1765, and his great-great grandson, Charles Dexter Ward, who returns to the village one hundred and ten years later with his wife Ann (Debra Paget). They are met with hostility by the villagers as they come to claim the mansion that is their inheritance, and only Dr. Willett is friendly, explaining the story of Joseph Corwen and telling of the horrible mutants which still roam the village, descendants of Curwen's abominable experiments. On reaching the castle, they are greeted by the evil manservant Simon Orme (Lon Chaney). Struck by a portrait of Curwen in the hall, Ward is soon possessed by Curwen's spirit, and, using Ward's body, Curwen and his warlock assistants, Orme and Jabez Hutchinson, go on with their plan to create a race of mutants which will take over the earth for the powers of darkness.

ABOVE *Vincent Price as the sadistic Mathew Hopkins in* Witchfinder General *(Tigon British 1968).*
BELOW *Getting ahead!* Devil's Nightmare *(Cetelci/Delfino 1971).*

LEFT *Vincent Price and Boris Karloff in the comedy-horror film* The Raven *(AIP 1963)*
RIGHT *Price threatens his faithless wife Barbara Steele in* The Pit and The Pendulum *(AIP 1961)*.

Diverted from this task by an obsession to revive the corpse of his dead sweetheart and also to exact revenge on the descendants of the men who killed him, Curwen leaves Ann aware of the terrible change that has overtaken her husband. Both she and Doctor Willett try to get him to leave. In a typical Cormanesque climax, the villagers, roused by the deaths in their midst, storm the mansion and burn it and the portrait. As the portrait is burned, Ward regains control of his body and saves Ann from sacrifice to the Dark Powers deep in the vault beneath the mansion. He, Ann and the Doctor escape the flames but in an equivocally frightening ending, we are not sure whether the man leaning wearily against the tree where Curwen was burned as a warlock is Curwen or Ward.

The Raven (US 1963) was a marvellous excuse for Corman to get Price, Karloff and Lorre together in an often frightening but always delightfully funny send-up of previous Corman-Poe adaptations. All that is left of Poe in Matheson's admirable script is the title and the final quotation 'Quoth the Raven, Nevermore!' From the moment a tetchy raven enters Dr. Craven's castle rasping out insults in Peter Lorre's familiar voice, to the duel of magic between Price's Dr. Craven and Karloff's Dr. Scarabus, the film is full of delightful and felicitous moments.

Seeking the potion which will transform the raven back into Lorre, Price opens his father's coffin to get some dead man's hair. For a moment the corpse comes to life as Price snips fastidiously at its locks, to grasp the son's arm and utter the whispered warning 'Beware!' before resuming its state of death. During the duel, Lorre is foolish enough to challenge the powers of Karloff once more—this time, instead of ending up as a bird, after a flash and a puff of smoke there is an ominous red pool on the stone floor where Lorre had been standing: Price goes over to it, looks at it quizzically, dips a finger, licks it and says, in his fruitiest voice: 'Ah! Raspberry jam!' The three principal actors carry the film on their ample shoulders.

Vincent Price also starred in Corman's first horror film in Britain, *The Masque of the Red Death*

ABOVE *Price and Jane Asher meet Death himself in* The Masque of The Red Death *(Alta Vista/Anglo Amalgamated 1964)*.

(GB 1964), a fascinating mixture of the sadistic and macabre, with Price in fine evil form as Prince Prospero, ruthless despot and Devil Worshipper. The film is filled with fine images of horror, elegantly filmed in luxurious colour by Nicolas Roeg. One memorable instance of this occurs when a dwarf, Hop Toad (Skip Martin) revenges himself on Alfredo (Patrick Magee) who has struck the tiny girl Esmeralda. His revenge is both bizarre and ghastly and pure film. Hop Toad persuades Alfredo to go to the masque dressed as a great ape. When the grotesque creature stumbles into the ballroom, it is seized by the dwarf, pinioned and hoisted up onto a candelabra—there to be saturated with brandy and set alight. The candelabra crashes to the floor and the man in the ape skin is incinerated.

The Masque of The Red Death is almost certainly Corman's finest film, with a sure control of tension and character evident in every scene. Price complements his vision with a deeply thoughtful performance as Prospero, evil incarnate, and yet with strange ambiguities of character, devising sadistic tortures with evident glee at one moment, yet pleading for the life of Francesca (Jane Asher) as Death comes to claim him at the final Masque. This is a sequence of carefully choreographed fear, as the red-robed and hooded figure of Death moves among the revellers, touching them so they sink lifeless among the slow gyrations of those about to die. And if Bergman has been imitated in the final scene when the various robed emissaries of death gather to report from the four corners of the earth, the imitation has been subtly altered and incorporated into the strictly private vision of horror that is Corman's alone.

As long as Baron Frankenstein and his imitators carry out their nefarious experiments, screen horror will continue to offer its share of madmen of every kind, deranged doctors and mad scientists, characters guaranteed to explore every avenue of terror. The last word on the subject belongs to Doctor Moreau, speaking on behalf of all cinema madmen when he declared: 'I took a gorilla and, working with infinite care, I made my first man!'

ALL CREATURES GREAT & SMALL

"Now the monster was hideous to behold—he was clothed with scales like a fish . . . he had wings like a dragon, feet like a bear and out of his belly came fire and smoke; and his mouth was as the mouth of a lion." John Bunyan

JOHN BUNYAN'S 'scenario' for a creature of terror has long since been improved and made more hideous by makers of horror films. Movie monsters of every conceivable kind—animal, mineral and vegetable, gigantic and ghastly, mutant and malevolent, minute and monstrous—have always formed a major part of screen horror as they smashed, crashed, crept, leapt, slithered and shocked their horrible paths through hundreds of films.

The screen's first 'monster' made its appearance at the very first public film show in Paris on the evening of December 28, 1895. Women who had paid one franc to see the Lumière Brothers' entertainment screamed in fear as the 'monster'—the locomotive 'star' of the film *Arrival of a Train at Ciotat Station*—appeared, about to rush at them from the screen and crush them beneath its all-too-real wheels! That audience witnessed not only the birth of the cinema but the appearance of its first monster in the first film of fright.

On the previous evening, Louis and Auguste Lumière and their father Antoine had given a preview of their show to an invited audience of prominent Parisians. Among them was Georges Méliès, at 34 a successful illusionist and magician and proprietor of the Théâtre Robert-Houdin for eight years. He was mesmerized by the Lumières' invention, hitting upon the idea of showing filmed interludes between his own live magical stage acts. His immediate offer to buy one of the film machines was refused by Antoine Lumière, even when Méliès raised the bidding to 10,000 francs. Méliès was told, with monumental lack of foresight on the part of Lumière père, to save his money for a better purpose since once the initial novelty of the cinema as a scientific toy had worn off, it could have no possible commercial future.

Undeterred, Méliès bought components from the Englishman R. William Paul and built his own camera equipment. One year later he had made over 70 short films of a conventional nature, many of them, such as *Card Party* and *Gardener Burning Weeds* being no more than filmed fragments of real life, following the pattern set by the Lumière brothers.

However, by sheer accident, Méliès was to discover the camera's ability to 'cheat'. One day he was filming traffic in the Place de L'Opéra when his camera jammed. After some time, Méliès got it running again and finished filming the scene. When he came to process the film, however, he was amazed to discover that the omnibus he had been filming when the camera stopped had miraculously turned into a hearse! The time taken to repair his equipment had been eradicated on film. Méliès soon took advantage of his accidental discovery of the camera's ability to create illusions and that same year he 'starred' in the macabre film of *The Vanishing Lady*. Méliès was seen to place a pretty girl in a chair, cover her with a cloak and then, apparently without a break, whip away the cloak to reveal only a grinning skeleton! From then on Méliès, the world's first director made more than 1500 films in twelve years before sinking into obscurity. He established all the basic 'rules' and tricks of the cinema of horror, some unsurpassed monsters, and even the incredible and horrific make-up that became the trademarks of all horror films to come.

Méliès relished playing the role of the Devil, first appearing as a gigantic bat which turned into His Satanic Majesty in *The Devil's Castle* (1896), a film replete with other monsters including living skeletons, ghosts and witches, and ending in a climactic exorcism of the Devil in a great cloud of smoke. And all this in a film that ran for less than three minutes! Using the same sets, he detached his devilish head and sent it floating in *The Laboratory of Mephistopheles*, and produced further ghoulish creatures in *The Haunted Castle*. He brought a statue to life in *Pygmalion and Galatea*, created a man with four heads in *The Many-Headed Man* in 1898, had ghosts and skeletons 'busied in most mysterious proceedings' in *The Cave of Demons* in 1898, and played the Devil again in *The Devil in a Convent*

LEFT *Richard Van Vleet fights for his life against Ben and his army of rats in* Ben *(Bing Crosby 1972).*

(1899). A 'giant bug' crawled over the sleeper in *A Midnight Episode* while in *The Man with the Rubber Head* (1901), Méliès was able to produce the apparently swelling head by moving his subject on rails nearer to the camera in a single tracking movement. Miniature monsters, too, appeared in *The Dancing Midget* (1902) while in *The Oracle of Delphi* (1903) a stone sphinx came to life.

But 1903 was the year that saw Edwin S. Porter's *The Great Train Robbery* from the United States, a film that was to revolutionize film-making. For those film-makers who were to follow Porter's example, there was to be a future; for Méliès, inextricably wedded to his stage background, theatrical presentation and fixed camera positions, *The Great Train Robbery* marked the beginning of his decline into repetition and obscurity. Porter supplied the first really effective close-up, creating a real involvement between film and audience. The stage tradition, with scenes played in front of the camera as if behind a proscenium arch, had received a bullet between the eyes. Nevertheless Méliès was to carry on filming for another ten years before he was finally forced out of the American market by Edison.

Before this, however, Méliès made his greatest masterpiece, showing it to the public for the first time in the fairground cinema in the Place du Trône in Paris.

A Trip to The Moon (1902) combined elements of Jules Verne's *From The Earth to The Moon*, H. G. Wells' *First Men in The Moon* and Méliès' own fantastic imagination. It traced the voyage of a group of top-hatted explorers from the Earth to the Moon and back again. In the film, the Moon itself became a 'monster' with a human face that screwed up in agony as the scientists' rocket, fired at it from a huge cannon, landed in its eye! The explorers' umbrellas became the first vegetable monsters as they took root in the Moon's soil and changed into gigantic mushrooms. The first creatures from another world appeared as grotesque 'Selenites' with whom the explorers do battle. Played by a troupe of acrobats the Selenites provided the genesis of many screen monsters, with their heads like mythical birds, carapace-like wings and the claws of giant lobsters. Struck by the explorers' umbrellas, they exploded into dust, only to spring up again in even greater numbers.

After *A Trip to The Moon* Méliès created only one more screen monster of any consequence, the genuinely horrifying Abominable Giant of The Snows which ate alive a member of the Polar Expedition featured in *The Conquest of the Pole*.

The cinematic debut of the man-made monster occurred with *Der Golem* which emerged from Germany in 1913 and which was given the US title of *The Monster of Fate*. The Golem was a giant man made of clay, brought to life by Rabbi Judah Low Ben Bezalel to help his people combat the persecution of Emperor Rudolph II in 16th-century Prague. Actor-writer-director Paul Wegener had heard of this legend while working on location in Prague and decided to make it the subject of his next film. Wegener himself played the giant clay man as well as co-writing the film with Henrik Galeen, and co-directing and producing it! The Golem, discovered in the rubble of the excavations of the site of an old synagogue, is sold to a dealer as a large stone statue. With the help of old cabalistic books, the antiquary brings the clay monster to life, unaware that the Golem should only be revived to perform noble deeds. Instead, the dealer opportunely uses the monster as his servant, and to guard his beautiful daughter. The monster, as is the way with all his kind, falls in love with the girl and, on a traditional rampage of terror in which he smashes his way through the streets, goes in pursuit of her, terrifying the populace. Bursting through glass doors he follows his quarry to the top of a tower. As the desperate girl snatches the Star of David from his chest he falls from the tower, shattering on the street below.

The Golem was the natural forerunner of movie monsters such as Frankenstein's creation, and in his appearances—Wegener was to return three times to the theme—the Golem established many of the traditions of the horror film.

The most effectively terrifying of all the versions of the Golem was *Der Golem: Wie Er in Die Welt Kam* (*The Golem: How He Came into the World*) (US Title: *The Golem*), which Wegener made in 1920. It was filmed in contorted, bizarre sets with strange uneven houses forming the ancient part of Prague.

The looming streets contrasted eerily with the Rabbi's chamber where he gave life to the Golem and to the girl's delicate bedroom. Towering over all was Wegener's Golem, stomping and smashing his way through alternate shadowed streets and sudden brightly lit scenes building up the horror by contrast. The film was photographed by Karl Freund, who was later to photograph Lugosi in *Dracula* and direct Karloff in *The Mummy*.

Horror and fear are created throughout the film, but several key scenes stand out, notably the dawn of life in the clay creature, with the Rabbi (Albert Steinruck) standing with his creation in a flaming circle, uttering one by one the mystic words to find the one that will bring life. The spirit of Astaroth appears and, letter by letter, the mystic word 'A-E-M-A-E-R' forms in smoke on his lips. The Rabbi writes the word and places it in the amulet on the clay man's chest. The Golem's eyes blaze—the creature is alive! The last scene mixes horror and genuine lyricism in a stupendous climax. The Rabbi's assistant, in love with the Rabbi's daughter (Lyda Salmanova), sends the Golem out to destroy his rival in love. Obligingly, the Golem seizes the luckless man and dashes him to his death from a tower. Soon he has set fire to the ghetto with a blazing log, and the scenes as the Golem, with the Rabbi's daughter cradled in his arms, lumbers his way through the terror-crazed crowds in the burning ghetto, bring frenzied, claustrophobic fear. Finally, the Golem is brought crashing lifeless to the ground by a small girl, who innocently offers the creature an apple, toys with the amulet, and finally removes the mystic word placed there by the Rabbi to give the Golem life. The Golem reappeared as *It* (1966), made in colour with Allan Sellars covering himself with Wegener's clay. Here a medieval statue is all that remains of a museum fire. Soon brought to life by Arthur Pimm (Roddy McDowall), It kills the new museum curator and, for the sheer delight of it, destroys Hammersmith Bridge as well! In the end the unfortunate Pimm is killed by a small nuclear bomb intended for the monster's destruction while, unharmed, the new Golem paddles off into the sea!

The fashion for giant animals was set by Willis H. O'Brien's special effects for the film of Sir Arthur Conan Doyle's *The Lost World* (US 1925). The direction of the human actors—Wallace Beery as Professor Challenger, Lewis Stone, Bessie Love, and Bull Montana as the Ape-Man—was indifferent and the cast no more than adequate.

However the film employed some fifty miniature dinosaurs and prehistoric lizards, built of rubber over wooden joints so that they could be filmed moving gradually against appropriately scaled-down backgrounds. The live actors were filmed separately, then reduced in size. The animated monster sequences and live action were then matched together to form one image. The overall effect was so realistic that the film was chosen as one of the year's Ten Best by the American Trade Journal *Motion Picture Daily*. Nobody went to *The Lost World* to see Beery, Stone or Love—the real stars were the prehistoric monsters slinking through jungles, battling among themselves, charging headlong in terror before an eruption of a

ABOVE *Creatures of the Imagination from George Méliès'* 2,000 Leagues Under the Sea *(Méliès 1906)*.
BELOW The Creeping Flesh *(Tigon British/World Film Services 1972)*.

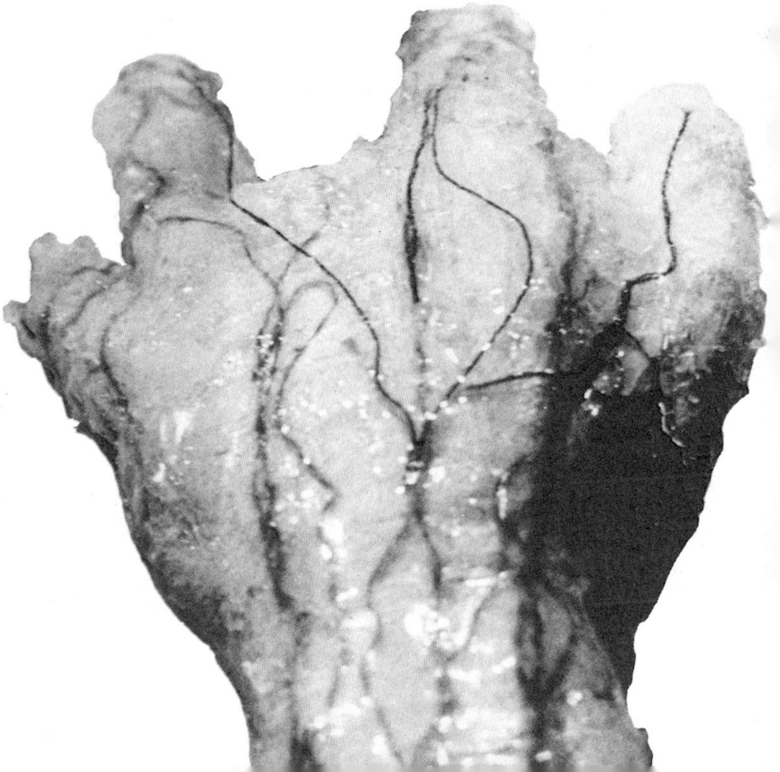

volcano, and finally, a live pterodactyl flapping its awesome way around a lecture hall in London, and an escaped brontosaurus running wild in the streets, ultimately bringing down Tower Bridge in ruins. The success of these monster stars was to be repeated through King Kong and up to the Japanese monster films of the Sixties and Seventies.

The greatest of all animal monster stars was an instant success. When *King Kong* opened simultaneously in 1933 at the world's then biggest cinema, The Music Hall at Radio City in New York's Rockefeller Centre, and at the nearby RKO Roxy, both cinemas were besieged with eager cinemagoers. The film was an instant world-wide success, and still commands huge audiences whenever it turns up again on television.

The concept of the film came from Meriam C. Cooper, up to then a notable documentary film maker with his colleague Ernest B. Shoedsack. On a location trip to Africa Cooper had become fascinated by gorillas, coming up with the idea for a film of a giant intelligent ape that would stampede through the streets of a modern world.

Once again, the human stars of *King Kong* lost out to the animals in every scene. Even the very accomplished screamer, Fay Wray, could do little to upstage a monster 50 feet high, with a face 7 feet from hairline to chin, embellished with ears 1-foot long, a 6-foot mouth when Kong smiled, a 2-foot nose and eyes a mere 10 inches across. His chest measured 60 feet (unexpanded), his legs 15 feet long, while his 23-foot long arms had a reach of 75 feet. It is little wonder that, faced with screen competition on this scale, Fay Wray contented herself with screaming her head off in between comfortable periods in a dead faint.

Stop-motion photography achieved the animation of Kong, for whom dozens of models were made varying in size and complexity for the required effect. They averaged sixteen inches high and were built of rubber and sponge material over articulated metal frames that permitted the limbs, eyes and mouth to move in order for them to be animated on film. The maximum day's work with the models would result in no more than half a minute of screen time photographed. When King Kong took Fay Wray up in his hand and examined her curiously, undressing her as decorously as the film permitted, the shot took 23 hours to complete. For such close-ups, full-scale models of Kong's hand and chest were built and the whole piece of film was made up from a combination of live-action with Miss Wray in the grip of the monster's hand, a smaller hand holding a doll-sized model, back projection, travelling mattes and the full range of available technical expertise. The result was a masterpiece of cinema monstrosity and special effects, yet so well integrated into the film that never for an instant was it in danger of being overwhelmed by special effects.

The film goes all out for the most outsize version possible of the theme of Beauty and the Beast. It begins with this theme openly stated in the form of 'An old Arabian Proverb—And the Beast looked upon the things of Beauty and lo! his hand was stayed from killing and from that day forward he was as one dead'. Kong provides some of the greatest monster mayhem to be seen on the screen.

Soon after his appearance, he first claps his 10-inch eyes on Fay Wray! She forms part of the expedition to Skull Island, in a mysterious area south-west of Sumatra, led by impresario Carl Denham (Robert Armstrong) along with an accompanying film unit. The natives, however, soon prove unfriendly, and in a scene of mounting terror Fay Wray is chained to two pillars to await her sacrifice to the mighty Kong, while Max Steiner's insistent score, the chanting of the native witch doctor and his people all build up to the first sight of Kong, come to claim his bride after five reels of almost unbearable suspense.

From the first great climax of Kong's appearance until the film's closing sequence, tension and horror never let up. In sheer frustration, Kong completely destroys the native village with crushing feet and blows from his fists which smash huts like egg shells. Kong then fights a tyrannosaurus while Fay Wray watches perched high up in a tree; later he battles with a pterodactyl and a giant snake. Finally captured by Driscoll (Bruce Cabot) with gas grenades, Kong later wreaks havoc in New York, hurling women from skyscrapers to their death on the pavements below, reducing a mighty civilization to the status of ants fighting a man.

His last magnificent battle is staged on top of the Empire State Building, swatting at attacking biplanes as though they were mosquitoes. Eventually, fatally weakened by this aerial onslaught he plunges 102 stories to his death.

Before O'Brien's next film, D. W. Griffith emerged briefly from Hollywood oblivion to direct the incredible prehistoric epic *One Million B.C./ Man and His Mate* (US 1940). This bizarre monster film told a story of everyday cavemen in their struggle against the dinosaurs and other monsters that trampled their world. The monsters in this case were no stop-frame creations of rubber and sponge with hair over articulated metal joints, but actual lizards locked in combat and challenging the

A giant among giant monsters. Willis O'Brien's King Kong *(RKO 1933).*

human actors. Because of their reality and the obvious pain of their battles together, the American Society for The Prevention of Cruelty to Animals found this type of monster too much to countenance and so an immediate ban on such 'creations' was imposed.

Nevertheless, these enlarged and suitably slowed down prehistoric monsters continued to appear in such other horror films as *Two Lost Worlds* (US 1951), *Robot Monster* (US 1953) and *King Dinosaur* (US 1954).

Griffith had his cavemen speaking impeccable English to each other, and when producer Hal Roach deleted all his spoken dialogue, dubbing instead a series of groans and grunts, Griffith insisted that his name be taken from the credits of the picture.

This marked Griffith's final attempt at film-making; the subject's great possibilities were not realized until Hammer's colour remake *One Million Years B.C.* (GB 1966) which incorporated a mixture of enlarged reptiles and some brilliantly conceived and animated monsters.

Monster films languished for a few years at the end of the Forties, to be reactivated in the Fifties with a cycle of films whose monsters came either

from Outer Space or were created as a result of insane or accidental tampering with the uncontrollable forces of atomic radiation. Horror and science fiction joined forces to create some of the most scaring of screen monsters which range from sentient jellies to giant tarantulas.

The first creature from another universe arrived in *The Day The Earth Stood Still* (US 1951), in the shape of the noble Klaatu (Michael Rennie) who brought his nine-foot robot Gort. The latter was programmed to destroy the world should the earth continue to make atomic tests. Klaatu is killed but not before he is befriended by a widow (Patricia Neal) to whom he passes on the mystic words 'Klaatu nikto barada' which she utters to switch off the robot. The world saved, Gort picks up Klaatu's body, enters their flying saucer and vanishes back into space. (Flying saucers were a popular mode of film transport at this time, following the world-wide flying saucer scares of the late Forties.)

A flying saucer also brought *The Thing From Another World* (US 1951), an eight-foot high 'intellectual carrot' (played by 6 foot 6 inches tall James Arnold). This creature fed on blood, grew extra limbs when dogs tore them off and propagated itself in an arctic army base by growing in true vegetable spirit, little 'things' which resembled giant pea pods but tended to wail 'like a newborn child'. After attacking huskie and human alike the thing is roasted in a trap of high voltage electricity. Ray Bradbury's *The Beast From 20,000 Fathoms* (US 1953), let loose a prehistoric monster to wreak havoc in a modern city. Woken by an atomic test it demolishes a lighthouse and is finally shot down by a missile containing radioactive isotopes as it destroys an amusement park, roller coaster and all. The monster is particularly convincing especially in its final scenes of destruction and death, set in a night lanced by searchlight beams.

The year 1954 became a vintage one for bizarre horrors ranging from *The Snow Creature* (US 1954), to the giant two-hundred-year-old frog in *The Maze* (US 1954), a perpetual burden to his heirs who had the task of looking after him in his ancestral Scottish castle home. This film was made in 3-D by William Cameron Menzies, the man responsible for the majestic special effects in the 1936 British film *The Shape of Things to Come.*

Walt Disney provided some giant and unpleasant underwater monsters for Kirk Douglas to battle in *Twenty Thousand Leagues Under the Sea* (US 1954), and atomic radiation produced lethal giant ants in *Them!* (US 1954). This film provided all the horror the audiences could desire, along with intelligent direction by Gordon Douglas, and convincing 15-foot ants loose in the New Mexico desert, killing their victims with mauling injections of concentrated formic acid! The horror of these monsters was accentuated by the almost documentary handling of the story, culminating in the eerie discovery and destruction of a nest of the giant ants in the depths of a storm drain, overlooked by a mental hospital whose patients had been raving unheeded about the monsters.

Jack Arnold made the first in the series of Gill Man monster pictures with *The Creature From The Black Lagoon* (US 1954). The Creature was designed by Universal's Bud Westmore and Jack Kevan after Arnold hit upon the basic idea for its appearance as he was sitting in his office.

ABOVE *Ricou Browning as the Gill Man carries Julia Adams in Jack Arnold's* Creature From the Black Lagoon *(Universal 1954).*
RIGHT *Jeremy Kemp is strangled by the creeping vine in Freddie Francis'* Dr. Terror's House of Horrors *(Amicus 1964).*

Ray Harryhausen's *monstrous creations from* The Valley of Gwangi *(Charles H. Schneer 1968). James Franciscus and a team of cowboys capture a giant prehistoric allosaurus, which, after decimating part of a Mexican city and battling with an elephant, finally dies in a blazing cathedral.*

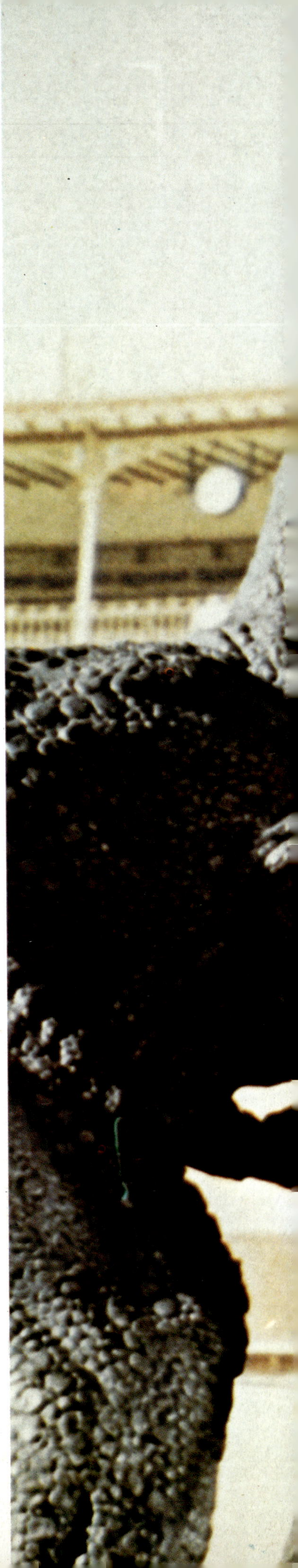

GWA

LEFT *The castaways battle with a giant crab in* Mysterious Island *(Columbia 1961).*
BELOW *Cowboys look on as the allosaurus and styracosaurus battle to the death in* The Valley of Gwangi *(Charles H. Schneer 1968).*
RIGHT *After* The Birds, *the insects attack mankind in* Genocide *(Shochiku 1968).*

He had spent some considerable time trying to devise a suitably terrifying monster without achieving what he wanted. The Gill Man, who was to 'star' in three pictures for Universal, finally evolved from a basic figure and a shape onto which Arnold had the designers graft the fins, flippers and nightmarish amphibian face. Swum by Ricou Browning, the Creature from the Black Lagoon entered the ranks of great Universal monsters. In the first of his screen appearances, he attacks and kills members of an Amazonian anthropological expedition, before reappearing downstream in the Black Lagoon to carry on his terrifying deeds, swimming after Julie Adams but finally to be overpowered by a drug injected into the water of the Lagoon. The Creature's first incarnation ends as he is shot and falls back into the water in the eerie underground cave where he has taken Julie Adams. Throughout the film, with its lucid underwater photography by James C. Havens, Arnold maintains an aura of fear and menace, making considerably more of the film than the 'conventional' monster film it might have turned out to be.

The Gill Man was sufficiently successful to warrant Arnold being pressed into making a sequel, the equally effective *Revenge of the Creature* (US 1955).

This time Arnold set the prehistoric monster in the stark white of a Miami aquarium and the panicked streets of the city. The creature prowls the night-time city seeking the heroine (Lori Nelson), and finally tracks her down in the night-club by the water. The Gill Man bursts into this garish scene, abducts the girl and plunges with her into the dark river. Trapped by his own need to re-enter the water every few minutes in order to obtain oxygen, the Gill Man is caught in the beams of the pursuers' searchlights. He is shot once more and sinks back dead into the water. Ricou Browning was called upon a second time to play the creature and the part demanded that he swim underwater, holding his breath as long as possible.

The Gill Man's final monstrous appearance without Arnold's guiding hand was in *The Creature Walks Among Us* (US 1956) where, after the experimentation of scientist Jeff Morrow, he escaped out to sea, ending the cycle of Gill Man pictures.

Britain's first successful international monster was Richard Wordsworth's mutating spaceman roaming London in *The Quatermass Experiment*, Hammer's adaptation of the riveting television serial by Nigel Kneale. Wordsworth played the sole, infected survivor from an abortive space shot, roaming London and bringing death with his touch, until finally he changes into a hideous non-human monster which meets its death by electrocution in Westminster Abbey!

Jack Arnold contributed a giant insect in *Tarantula* (US 1955), a spider the size of an office block, which Leo G. Carroll creates when using artificial nutrients in experiments to increase animal growth and so solve the world's food problems. (Arnold took this theme from a documentary film he made for US Department of Agriculture about the experimental feeding of chickens to produce 'super fowls' with more meat!) After devastating the countryside around Carroll's laboratory, crunching cars in his mandibles, Tarantula is finally burned to death by jet planes dropping napalm upon it. Arnold's handling of this, plus superior special effects from Universal, make *Tarantula* as terrifying a monster as *Them!* with the extra frisson of an almost universal terror of spiders.

In 1956 came *Godzilla*, the first of many films of the monster genre from Toho's Inishiro Honda. Godzilla, although promoted as making 'King Kong look like a Midget!' was in reality a man in reptile's clothing! The painstaking miniature sets and special effects of Eiji Tsuburuya gave Godzilla, even in his unanimated incarnation, all the power and terror associated with a 'classical' giant monster.

Looking like a cross between a dragon and some

prehistoric nightmare, Godzilla is awakened by the atomic explosion on Bikini Atoll. Literally breathing fire—a lethal ray jetted out of his mouth—the 400 foot high monster attacks and nearly destroys all Tokyo. No conventional weapon proves effective against him as he tramples the city to fragments, picking up railway trains and crunching them between his teeth, enjoying the apparently pleasant stimulus of high-voltage electricity. Finally it was left to the cunning Japanese, the one people who had suffered under the terror of a real atomic attack, to destroy Godzilla with the ultimate atomic weapon, wielded by its perfector, an idealistic scientist who gave his life to kill the monster. The commercial success of the film outside Japan, with Raymond Burr giving an interpolated running commentary on the action while Japanese actors were dubbed into American, was so enormous that Honda and Toho provided Godzilla with almost as many reincarnations as the Frankenstein Monster!

Godzilla, constantly being done to death in the final reel, emerged time and time again, to take on any other monster that Toho could find to match him against. King Kong (this time animated from within by the Kong suit's wearer) was the first major adversary in *King Kong Versus Godzilla* (Japan 1963). Godzilla emerges from a giant radioactive iceberg while King Kong is captured on his Pacific Island home, but not before doing battle with a giant octopus. Escaping from the raft which is towing him back to Japan, Kong escapes and heads towards Japan to do battle with his enemy Godzilla. Their first meeting is brief, with Kong retreating from the radioactive halitosis of the giant reptile's breath! Finally, after both monsters have caused more than the usual ration of destruction and carnage, they meet for one final apocalyptic confrontation. At first it looks like a clear victory for Godzilla, but old monsters die hard and, rejuvenated by an electrical storm, Kong wades into the upstart reptile until, at the height of the battle, there is an earthquake which precipitates both monsters over a cliff into the sea! In traditional manner, the victorious King Kong wades off into the sunset, striding into the sea back to his remote island home.

The reports of Godzilla's death were greatly exaggerated, however, and he was back again in *Godzilla versus the Thing* (Japan 1964) in which after his usual rampage, Godzilla fights and beats the giant moth Mothra, before being toppled off a

BELOW LEFT *Grant Williams battles for his life in Jack Arnold's horror masterpiece* The Incredible Shrinking Man *(Universal 1957)*.
BELOW RIGHT *The formless monster from space attacks Japan in* Space Amoeba *(Toho 1970)*.

cliff by Mothra's two monstrous caterpillar progeny who cover Godzilla with a shroud of silk in their final battle! Revived by a lightning conductor which awakens him when the next thunderstorm passes overhead, Godzilla is on the side of Good in *Ebirah—Terror of The Deep*, despite an initial orgy of city-smashing and pyrotechnics, when he destroys not only the giant lobster of the title, but throws in the destruction of the fiendish Red Bamboo who seek world domination! *Son of Godzilla* (Japan 1967) showed the reptile to be a fine family monster. Alone Godzilla despatches a quartet of enormous praying mantises, while father and son join forces to kill off the gigantic spider Spigon. After such magnificent achievements, in a picture beautifully constructed and containing superb special effects from Eiji Tsuburaya, the Godzilla family are only too happy to huddle together and enter a state of frozen hibernation.

In 1968 Godzilla made a return appearance to join the party of monsters in *Destroy All Monsters!* Set in 1999, Godzilla leads all the Toho monsters in a battle against a hydra-headed creation, Ghidorah, and a flying saucer sent flaming against Godzilla and his allies by the evil aliens from the planet Kilaak. The climactic confrontation, in which the forces of Good and Godzilla vanquish the extra-terrestrial King Ghidorah, takes place on Mount Fuji, watched with clapping approval by Son of Godzilla.

Toho's giant monsters lack in some respects the technical cleverness of stop-motion animation, relying instead on less complex animation and on monsters operated by people inside them. Photographed against brilliantly designed and executed model cities and harbours, however, they have won world-wide success which makes them like all really effective horror films, basically critic-proof.

With *The Incredible Shrinking Man* (US 1957), Jack Arnold made his masterpiece of horror which turned the conventions of the screen monster upside-down. Instead of normal man locked in combat with giant creatures loose in his own comfortably familiar environment, replete with all the armoury of modern science and technology, the incredible shrinking man found himself in an alien environment, matched against 'giant' monsters who had once been pets and insects of his everyday life.

The plot, written from his own novel by Richard Matheson, is deceptively simple. Scott Carey (Grant Williams) is sunbathing on the roof of his cabin cruiser when a patch of mist suddenly comes

BELOW LEFT *The Brown Gargantua and the Green Gargantua battle over Tokyo in* The War of the Gargantuas *(Toho 1967).*
BELOW RIGHT *Battersea funfair comes under attack from Gorgo's mother in* Gorgo *(King Bros. 1960).*

up and envelops the boat. Carey's body is covered with silver scales which rapidly vanish, apparently without any adverse effect.

Six months later, however, Carey finds himself beginning to shrink. The first intimation, a moment of pure cinema horror, comes when his wedding ring suddenly slips from his finger onto the floor of his car. After that, his situation rapidly becomes worse—his clothes become too large, his relationship with his wife deteriorates and, unable to be helped by science, he shrinks to three feet high, to be exploited as a nine-day wonder by the media, then abandoned as a freak. He finds a brief moment of human happiness with a circus midget who accepts him as another human being and not a freak, but as he becomes smaller, she too becomes a 'giant' to him. Six inches high, he is reduced to living in a doll's house in his living room, but this relative haven becomes a place of terror when he is attacked by his erstwhile family pet, a cat now assuming gigantic proportions, snarling and spitting at the windows of the doll's house, playing with him as it would with a mouse, until the monster chases him into the cellar. Believing that the cat has killed her husband, Carey's wife abandons him to a nightmare existence in the deserted cellar of the house.

Shrinking even further, living from drops of water from a leaking cistern, Carey fights a spider for a piece of stale bread which is his only food.

Few screen monsters have matched the horror of the giant spider, shaken from its web by Carey, who has to kill it or die from starvation. Their fight, ending with Carey 'harpooning' the creature with a bent pin attached to a piece of thread tied to a pair of scissors, has an epic quality of terror, ended only when the scissors are pushed off a ledge to drag the impaled insect down to the floor. Carey finally slips from the 'normal' world to a new existence somewhere in the unknown.

The atom-haunted Fifties went out in a blaze of screen monsters ranging from enlarged insects amok in the English countryside in *The Strange World of Planet X* (GB 1958); the snarling rubbery Martian monster in *The Terror From Beyond Space* (US 1958); *The Trollenberg Terror* (GB 1958), tentacled brain-like creatures with staring eyes who lived in their own radioactive cloud high on a Swiss mountain; the encrusted abnormality found in Pompeiian ruins who dissolved in the sea while making off with a beautiful artist in *Curse of The Faceless Man* (US 1958); to Ray Harryhausen's bizarre and horrible mythical creatures populating *The 7th Voyage of Sinbad* (US 1958), which include a dragon, two-headed rocs, a four-armed dancing snake-woman, a man-eating cyclops and a duelling skeleton.

The Sixties, while indeed less preoccupied with the menace of atomic experimentation, provided a smaller but equally ripe crop of creatures great and small. George Pal's time travellers met up with the repellently hairy future mutants, the Morlocks, in *The Time Machine* (US 1960). *Konga* (GB 1960) provided a diet of carnivorous plants and a gigantified chimpanzee who virtually destroyed London, including that most popular of targets for giant monsters, the tower of Big Ben.

For sheer imagination if somewhat limited activities, the Japanese monsters of the Sixties and Seventies seem to outshine their Western counterparts who tend to stick to standard prehistoric monsters.

Toho gave birth to the scaly, spikey-spined prehistoric *Varan the Unbelievable* which sank a couple of ships, snapped up and ate an aircraft and knocked down a remarkably self-generating Tokyo before swallowing explosive and dying. Then came the giant flying monster *Mothra*, humanoid mushrooms in *Matango, Fungus of Terror*, a gargantuan monster sea-snake in *Atragon*, while in *Gappa*, the title monster, amphibious, bird-like and evidently jet-propelled in some mysterious fashion, is hatched by a giant octopus.

In 1966 came Hammer's new *One Million Years B.C.* (GB 1966) with some especially fine monsters from Ray Harryhausen. Filmed in colour, it brilliantly achieved all that the first version had failed to create. One after another, monsters fill the screen—a giant lizard, a brontosaurus and an enormous turtle. There is one of the best-staged prehistoric battles between a triceratops and a ceratosaurus and, as a pièce de resistance, a huge pterodactyl swoops off with Raquel Welch to offer the scantily-clad Shell Lady to its snapping fledglings! There have been few more fortunate monsters in the history of screen horror!

The horror movie monster is certainly one of the most varied of all creations of the cinema of terror and continues to be one of the most popular. Man's wildest imaginings can, through the power of the cinema, become only too real, and the witches, demons and evil spirits of childhood and a less scientific age have been replaced by the multitude of movie monsters, large and small, prehistoric and interplanetary, which have made their fearsome way across cinema screens since Méliès, the Wizard of Montreuil, first turned his camera into a machine of illusion, mystery and horror.

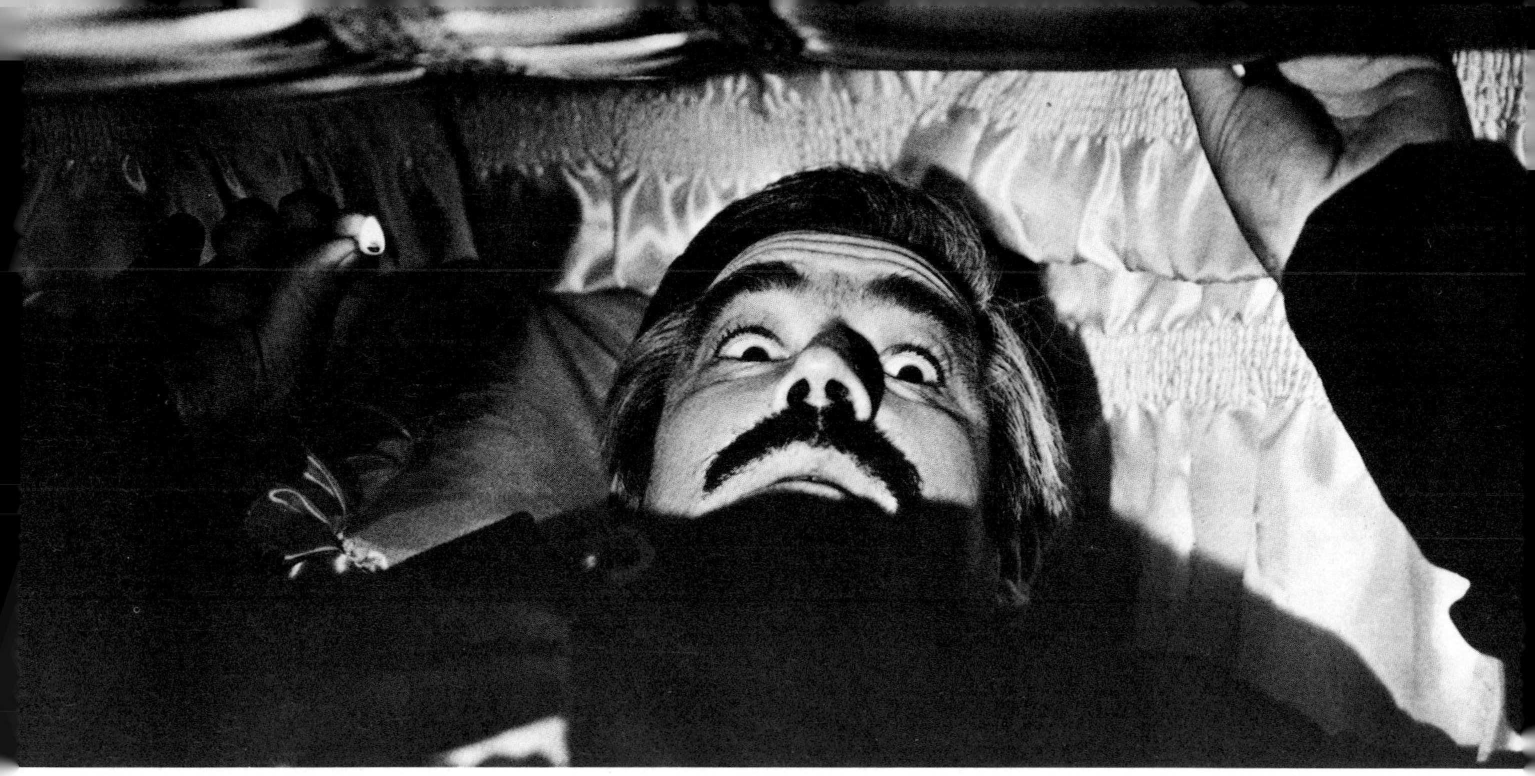

ABOVE *The End? Michael Craig awakens from a feigned death to find himself buried alive in* Vault of Horror *(Metromedia/Amicus 1973).*

ACKNOWLEDGMENTS

The author would like to express his gratitude to the following people and organizations who gave encouragement, time and assistance in providing information and material invaluable in the preparation of this book:

Mr Jack Arnold, Mr Peter Cushing, Mr Christopher Lee, Sir James Carreras, Mr Michael Carreras, Mr Peter Duffell, Mr Terence Fisher, Mr Jimmy Sangster, Mr Freddie Francis, Mr Kevin Francis, Mr Roy Ashton, Mr Herman Cohen, Mr Carlos Clarens, Mr Anthony Nelson Keys, Mr Robin James, Mr Leslie Halliwell, Mr David Golding, Mr Ken Ferguson, Mr Eric P. Greenspan (Ember Film Distributors), Mr John Phillips (Butcher's Film Distributors), Mr L. Pound and Mr Dennis Michael (CIC [UK]), Mr Milton Subotsky (Amicus Productions), Miss Lily Poyser, Mrs Carol Futrall, Mr W. G. Chalmers (Doverton Films), Mr Charles Berman (United Artists), Mr John Troke (Anglo EMI Film Distributors), Mr Michael Buist (EMI Film Distributors), Mr Charles H. Schneer (Ameran Films), The Italian Chamber of Commerce For Great Britain, Mr Peter A. Clark (LMG Film Distributors), Cinerama Releasing (UK), Mr Neil Agran (Target International), Mr Peter L. Andrews (Chilton Films), Mr John Daly and Mr John Hogarth (Hemdale), Mr M. J. G. Fancey (New Realm), Mr Peter Jacobs (Paladin Films), Mr H. Chujo (Shochiku Co. Ltd., Japan), Mr Milton Moritz (AIP), Omnia Deutsche Film Export G.M.B.H., The Japanese Trade Centre, London, Mr Maurice King (King International Corporation), Mr H. Noune (Toho International), The Staff of all departments of the British Film Institute and National Film Archive.

The stills from *Countess Dracula, Twins of Evil* and *Vampire Circus* were supplied by courtesy of The Rank Organization Limited.

The stills from *The Beast Must Die* and *The Wicker Man* were supplied by courtesy of British Lion Films.

The stills from *The Curse of the Fly* and *The Return of the Fly* were supplied by courtesy of Twentieth Century-Fox.

Special picture research by John Kobal.

My thanks are owed to all the many individuals, too numerous to mention by name, who generously gave me the pick of their stills collections and ran films to enable me to refresh my memory of many happy ghoulish horror film moments.

This book is for Maggie, and for Kate and Liza.

FRONT ENDPAPERS *Christopher Lee prepares to make a sacrifice of Joanna Lumley in* The Satanic Rites of Dracula *(Hammer 1973).*

BACK ENDPAPERS *Charlton Heston fights for his life against the Living Dead in* The Omega Man *(Seltzer 1971).*

INDEX OF FILM TITLES

Page numbers in italics refer to illustrations

GENERAL INDEX

Page numbers in italics refer to illustrations

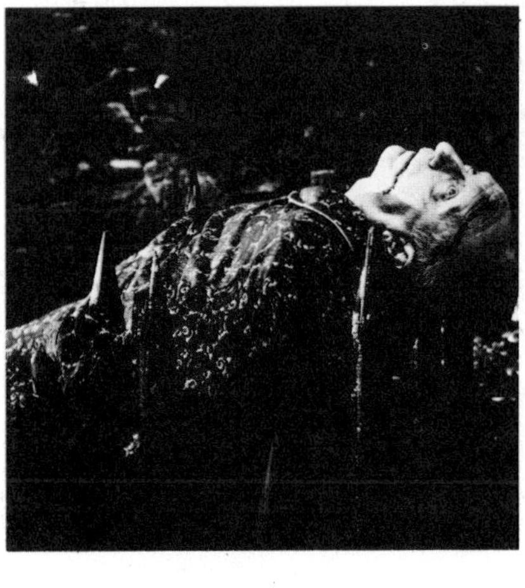

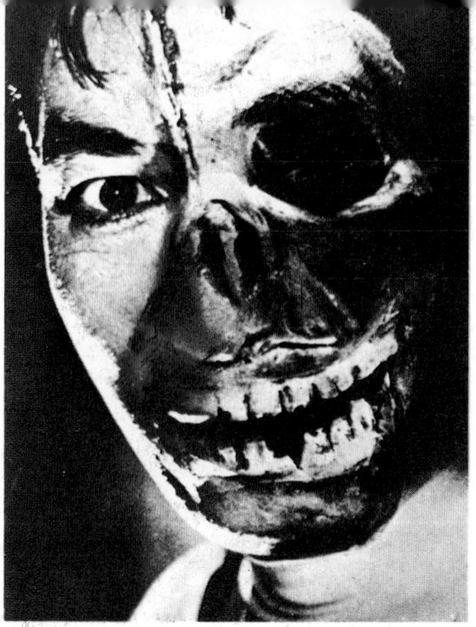

First published by Octopus Books Limited
This edition published by Cathay Books
59 Grosvenor Street, London W1

ISBN 0 86178 091 4

Printed in Hong Kong